CONTENTS

EDITORIAL

Stirling Moss: Britain's Greatest Racing Driver

MOSS: THE GREATEST

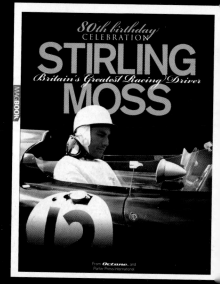

The greatest racing driver Britain has ever known? Or even, as motor racing historian Doug Nye claims in his wonderfully personal piece on Sir Stirling on pages 6-16, the greatest living Englishman? I think he has fair claim to both.

Going by results alone, of course, Stirling Moss doesn't cut it, but it was his hard-charging, heroic style, his no-nonsense personality and his way with the ladies that endeared him to the hearts of the general public, rather than just the motor racing fans.

And now of course, we know Stirling as the one racing hero who can be relyed upon to be open and friendly at all manner of public events, wife Susie always at his side, pen always poised to sign yet more autographs. Or, if he's not mingling with his fans, he's out there on the track, still in love with the cut and thrust of racing after all these years.

So here we celebrate Sir Stirling Moss in the year of his 80th birthday, a remarkable 47 years since the terrible Goodwood accident that forced him to retire from professional racing.

Read on, and decide for yourself if Stirling is 'Britain's Greatest Ever Racing Driver', or better…

David Lillywhite

David Lillywhite

'It was his heroic style and way with the ladies that endeared him to the public'

In association with

Porter Press International

Editorial office
Octane, 1 Tower Court, Irchester Road,
Wollaston, Northants NN29 7PJ, UK
Tel: +44 (0)207 907 6585. Fax: +44 (0)1933 667309
info@octane-magazine.com, www.octane-magazine.com

Advertising office
Octane Media Advertising Dept, 19 Highfield Lane,
Maidenhead, Berkshire SL6 3AN, UK
Tel: +44 (0)1628 510080. Fax: +44 (0)1628 510090
ads@octane-magazine.com, www.octane-magazine.com

Porter Press International
PO Box 2, Tenbury Wells,
Worcestershire, WR15 8XX, UK
Tel: +44 (0)1584 781588. Fax: +44 (0)1584 781630
info@porterpress.co.uk, www.porterpress.co.uk

Editors:	David Lillywhite
	Philip Porter
Designer:	Phil Long
Picture research:	Abigail Humphries
Production:	Nigel Grimshaw
	Sarah Bradley
	Richard Gunn
Editorial assistance:	Claire Bryan
PA to Philip Porter:	Mary Fulford-Talbot
Advertising director:	Sanjay Seetanah
Advertising sales:	Rob Schulp
Advertising production:	Anisha Mogra
Publishing director	Geoff Love
Newstrade director	Martin Belson
Marketing manager	Juliette Cooper
Managing director	Ian Westwood
Group finance director	Ian Leggett
COO	Brett Reynolds
CEO	James Tye
Chairman	Felix Dennis

Licensing
To license this product, please contact Winnie Liesenfeld on +44 (0) 20 7907 6134 or winnie_liesenfeld@dennis.co.uk

MAGBOOK
The 'Magbook' brand is a trademark of Dennis Publishing Ltd

Stirling Moss: Britain's Greatest Racing Driver is published under licence from Octane Media Ltd, a subsidiary company of Dennis Publishing Limited, United Kingdom. All rights in the licensed material belong to Felix Dennis, Octane Media, Dennis Publishing or Porter Press and may not be reproduced, whether in whole or in part, without their prior written consent. *Octane* is a registered trademark.

Repro by Octane Repro **Printed by** BGP, Bicester

Distribution Seymour, 2 East Poultry Avenue, London EC1A 9PT. Tel: +44 (0)20 7429 4000

Periodicals Postage paid @ Emigsville, PA. Postmaster: send address corrections to Octane Media c/o 33 Pacific Ave, Suite 404, Virginia Beach, VA 23451

Stirling Moss: Britain's Greatest Racing Driver ISSN 1906-372 published by Octane Media Ltd and Porter Press.

CONTRIBUTORS

STIRLING MOSS
Without Sir Stirling's help, this publication wouldn't exist. His never-ending enthusiasm and energy comes across in every article.

SUSIE MOSS
Lady Moss, always at Stirling's side, and an invaluable help in compiling the articles in this publication, airs her own views on page 140.

PHILIP PORTER
The vast majority of the features here have been written by Philip, who has just released the fourth in his series of Moss 'Scrapbooks'..

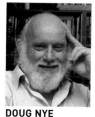

DOUG NYE
We have Stirling to thank for historian Doug's lifelong obsession with motor racing. He describes why on pages 6-16.

MARK DIXON
Octane magazine's deputy editor drove Stirling's legendary '722' Mercedes 300SLR just before it was put away for good – see p30.

Mon ami

MOSS

**World renowned motor racing historian Doug Nye suspects
that his entire life has been influenced by Stirling Moss,
from his childhood adoration to current close friendship**

Words: Doug Nye

Photography: The GP Library, The David Weguelin Collection,
The Hill Family Collection, *Motorfilms Quarterly*

I don't wish to alarm Stirl, but in many ways my entire life is down to him. No – not a cue for (another?) paternity suit – just a statement of fact, because he was the personality who riveted my infantile attention upon motor racing, which has since been entirely at the core of my being. Apparently when I was only five or six I would waffle on about 'Stirly Moss'. I couldn't pronounce his name any better. I kept hearing on the radio that 'Stirly Moss' had won here, and then 'Stirly Moss' had won there. I remember seeing pictures of The Boy and his racing cars in Mum and Dad's newspapers, and on both the editorial and advertising pages of *The Radio Times, Picture Post* and even – occasionally – in my big brother's (faintly naughty) magazines…

Brother Rod would return home from school to explode into incandescent rage at five-year-old me. I had just sawn up his square-section aeromodelling balsa wood to create straw bales for my Dinky Toy racing cars. I would use these balsa bales to mark out a track around the smooth kitchen-floor lino, then spin and crash and race my cars there for hour after hour. And in my tiny mind I was usually 'Stirly Moss', the demon driver, although I must confess that once I'd acquired the Dinky Toy Cooper-Bristol I sometimes morphed mentally into Mike Hawthorn: The Farnham Flyer – our local ace from up the road. But overall I was more a Moss kid than a Hawthorn fan. Sad but true, I was imprinted.

It is sad isn't it, how a 63-year-old can confess such childhood fantasies, but right now it's appropriate. Dammit, I was not alone. How many other young just-postwar Brits grew up with the same fevered imaginings? I wasn't seduced by Stirl advertising Craven-A cigarettes, but it was the racing and the winning – the winning for Britain as it was described at the time – which twanged my neurones.

I first got to know 'Golden Boy', as our late mutual friend Denis Jenkinson christened him, in the '70s and '80s. When I first got into motor racing in the 1960s I'd always been too much in awe even to dare speaking to him. I remember seeing him push-started in a Maserati 250F at Silverstone for some historic demo, and stalling it immediately. So the first words I actually heard the legendary Stirling Moss utter were 'Oh *bugger*!'

On a new car launch somewhere in snowy Switzerland we shared a breakfast table, and began to laugh a lot. We hit it off. Years later he 'phoned and came down to see us which fazed me completely – why would Golden Boy want to visit me, rather than summon me to his Mayfair house? But upon arrival he explained he'd had an idea for a book about all the cars he'd ever raced – would I write it with him? Of course, I jumped at the chance. Apparently that process, with my prompting him with facts and photographs, helped rebuild his damaged memory. For years he addressed my wife as 'Mrs Doug' – now it's 'Valerie' and – what's more – he's got it right.

He's always been disarmingly honest. His opinions never sway just to make a newfound sponsor happy. His regard for Fangio as the greatest racing driver he ever saw endures undiminished, and when asked if he would like to have raced in the modern era – when his Schumacher-style earnings must surely have surmounted the hundreds of millions – he is disarmingly direct: 'No Boy, the money might be nice – but we had such a better time and a so much more enjoyable life style that I'm completely happy with what I've had.' His vivid directness could be evidence of superficiality. He is certainly totally apolitical. Artifice is not his way. But he can in fact be a deep thinking man, and one of surprising sensitivity. One year at the Goodwood Festival of Speed I saw a mum thank him for signing her little boy's autograph book. 'Oh no need for thanks my dear,' he said, 'You see this is my office and this is my day job.' Which spoke volumes.

Way back then, when I was ten, I remember the radio commentary upon the British Grand Prix and Grand Prix d'Europe being run somewhere up north called Aintree. I knew enough then to be aware that Moss was driving with World Champion Fangio in the Mercedes-Benz factory team while Hawthorn was driving for the Italian Ferrari 'équipe' – but for years Stirl our hero had refused to drive for these foreign outfits – he had compromised his own career by steadfastly driving British cars when not one was worthy.

This hadn't been so with the rival hero in my childhood fandom. Mike Hawthorn had been offered a Ferrari drive for 1953 and had grabbed the chance with both enormous hands. What's more he had promptly beaten Fangio to win the

Left and below
Mike Hawthorn and Moss at Silverstone, 1958; in action, 1961; Stirling enjoys the acclaim as winner of the 1955 Mille Miglia.

Above
Rare colour shot of the first Goodwood meeting, Moss poised to score his first big circuit-race win in the Cooper-JAP 500.

French Grand Prix! I clearly recall the fuss, but so sparse was UK coverage of Grand Prix racing at that time – unless some poor chap had been killed – that I had no idea my man Moss had floundered as his home-grown, flag-waving Cooper-Alta proved hopeless. Hawthorn might have sold out to Italy, our former enemy – as all the boy's comics of the time were still reminding us – but at Grand Prix level Moss was simply bashing his head against a stone wall.

Why should he be doing that? He had been born into motor racing. His father, Alfred, was a dentist, running a string of surgeries in the poorer parts of London. He would say he didn't need middle-class patients expecting conversation – 'Just get 'em in, Boy, yank, and take the money!' His commercial genes were to prove hereditary. His son built a reputation for rapt attention to the bottom line. 'Pa' Moss had raced Crouch cars at Brooklands and a Fronty-Ford in the Indy '500'. His wife Aileen was an expert trials driver in the 1930s. They encouraged fitness and competitiveness in their children, Stirling and sister Pat, who grew up surrounded by quality cars. But despite being naturally athletic Stirling suffered nephritis – a kidney ailment – and chronic ear-ache which cost much schooling. He had also been splashed with burning paraffin when larking about in a tree house, and he had developed both a

high tolerance of pain, and remarkable powers of recovery from injury. 'I was hopeless academically,' he recalls, '…and at 17 began work at the Palmerston Hotel as commis waiter. At the Eccleston Hotel in Victoria I discovered that if you collected the dregs from splits like bitter lemon or tonic water you quickly ended up with a bottle of your own to sell for a clear profit!'

Ever after, Moss the businessman retained a keen awareness of profit. But he always delivered, whether behind the steering wheel or on the celebrity circuit. Book Moss from 12 'til 3 and he would report for duty at 11:59, perform out of his boots on the client's behalf until the due time, and by 3:01 would be gone. The invoice would follow instantly. A fair day's work for a fair day's pay – another lifelong legacy from 'Pa' Moss.

Stirling had begun riding a Coventry Eagle motorcycle as a kid, and a 1936 Matchless-engined Morgan three-wheeler followed, then an MG PB Tickford Coupe, and in the winter of 1946-47 a BMW 328, in which 'Pa' allowed him to compete in club trials. He took a first-class award in the 1947 Eastbourne Rally – his first 'big win' – and also ran in the Speed Trials at Brighton and Poole, and sprinted on Merston aerodrome, near to Chichester… and to Goodwood.

He had read about the new Cooper-JAP 500 racing cars

being built by the Cooper Car Co in Surbiton, and badgered his Dad into helping him buy one for his 18th birthday. 'I'd saved a fair amount of money from my gymkhana prizes, but now had to sell my tent, radio, camera and so on. I think Dad bought them, but he had made his point – if I wanted something sacrifices were necessary – and believe me, he drove a hard bargain!'

Through 1948 the Moss family team towed their ivory-white Cooper around available events behind their pre-war Rolls-Royce 'Woody' estate, and The Boy shone. He won aerodrome circuit races at Brough, the inaugural Goodwood and Silverstone. He became a star of 500cc racing through 1949, and with a 1000cc JAP twin-cylinder engine finished third behind two Ferraris in his first Continental race, at Lake Garda in Italy. He was just 19 and the Italian *tifosi* loved him and his spidery little car. 'They christened it The Jukebox! I won £200, which was huge for those days and was a major step in my development from being an enthusiastic amateur towards proper professionalism.'

In fact the Italian racing establishment instantly accepted 'Steerleeny Moce' as a genuine talent while at home he was regarded with something approaching suspicion – a precocious hard-charger bound surely to hurt himself. The exceptions were hard-bitten racers George Abecassis and John Heath, who invited him to drive for their 1950 HWM team. They contested a full season of Formula 2, and Stirling's

reputation blossomed Internationally. But at Naples a local back-marker barged him off course into a roadside tree. He broke his knee and lost teeth. One injury was plastered, the other fixed by 'Pa', and he very quickly resumed racing.

He was desperate for a drive in Britain's biggest race – the Tourist Trophy at Dundrod in Ulster, but no manufacturer would consider him. He was still regarded as a risk. Nobody wanted their brand name to be associated with this meteoric new boy really hurting himself. Motoring writer Tommy Wisdom then loaned him his alloy-bodied Jaguar XK120. Stirl drove it in his first real sports car race, on a fiendishly daunting circuit, in pouring rain, he led most of the way, and won!

He was on his way, in demand, and his serious career as a professional racing driver was launched. He drove for Jaguar, and Aston Martin, the Rootes Group and BRM. He was courted by the media, and the emergent advertising world. Insistent upon driving British at Grand Prix level he was really trying to push water uphill. 'During 1953 Mercedes-Benz announced they were building a new Grand Prix car for 2½-litre Formula 1 racing in '54. My father, Ken Gregory – who handled my business affairs – and some motoring journalist friends suggested to Alfred Neubauer of Mercedes that I was worth considering for his new team. He – quite rightly – told them I had too little experience of really powerful cars and should first prove myself amongst the big

'The Italian racing establishment instantly accepted Moss as a genuine talent while at home he was regarded with suspicion'

Clockwise from above
With Joan Chambers at the 1950 premiere of *To Please a Lady*; Lago Di Garda with Cooper 1000.; with manager Ken Gregory and Mr and Mrs Dan Glover, who donated Goodwood's famous Glover Trophy for F1 racing there.

boys in a really competitive car, like one of the new Maseratis. I was in America when I heard that my family were ordering me a new 250F, Dad guaranteeing the cost of £5500... though it would be my money which would pay for it!'

In fact Stirling then shone in the Maserati, by mid-season was absorbed into the Italian factory team, and by the end of the year was regarded as their *de facto numero uno*. Neubauer then invited him to join Mercedes for 1955, Stirling jumped at the chance, and Maserati felt jilted. Eighteen months earlier, Fangio had made the same move. Stirl then learned in the Maestro's wheel tracks through '55. Winning the British Grand Prix at Aintree broke his duck. In Mercedes sports cars he proved supreme, winning the Mille Miglia, the Dundrod TT and the Targa Florio. And so he was on his way as absolutely one of the world's top racing drivers. He worked at every aspect of the job, every earning opportunity was addressed. He simply clicked with a global public way beyond motor racing fans.

Clockwise from top
Moss celebrates winning the 1955 TT; Phil Hill's shot of Vanwall boss Tony Vandervell; with Jenks in Mercedes '722' on the way to their historic 1955 Mille Miglia victory.

Fangio remained the contemporary top dog and standard-setter – but Moss's stature was growing in The Old Man's wake. He would be runner-up to Fangio – whom he adored – in the Drivers' World Championships of 1955-56-57, and was then just pipped by a solitary point to finish second again to compatriot Mike Hawthorn in 1958.

And perhaps his defeat by Mike that year was typical not only of the era, but also of Moss the Man. He explains: 'In the Portuguese GP at Oporto I was leading in the Vanwall and had set fastest lap, which scored an extra Championship point, when behind me Mike took second place and in the process lapped faster still. David Yorke – our Vanwall team manager – signalled me 'HAW-REC' which unfortunately I misread as 'HAW-REG', meaning 'Hawthorn – Regular', so not a threat. I lapped Mike just before the end, but the sight of his face as I did so softened my hard old heart, so I backed off and let him unlap himself. As we came up to the timing

Clockwise from above
Hawthorn gives Stirling the finger
at the RAC Champions party, 1958;
winning the Monaco GP in the Lotus 18,
1961; crowd-pleasing landmark victory
at the 1957 British GP in the Vanwall.

'I cursed the luck which had confined me to runner-up in the World Championship, but later came to realise it didn't matter'

line, he started his last lap just before I crossed it to win. To qualify for his second place he still had to complete that final lap, but he promptly spun and stalled.

'I came upon his stalled car on my slowing-down lap and saw him struggling to restart it in the direction of the race – uphill. I slowed beside him and bawled "Push it downhill; you'll never start the bloody thing that way!" Which he did, then swung it round and took the flag. Under the regulations, you could be disqualified for proceeding against the race direction, and after the race Mike was hauled before the stewards and I appeared as a witness for the defence. I testified that he had not been on the circuit at all when he proceeded against the race direction because he had been on the pavement instead. And they swallowed that, and confirmed his second place, and his extra point for fastest lap. And that's what bloody well sank me in the end! I am sure I could have taken that record lap back if only I had realised.

'But I've never regretted testifying on his behalf. It was the right thing to do. I cursed the luck which had confined me to runner-up in the World Championship for the fourth consecutive season – but though it mattered like hell at the time, I later came to realise it didn't really matter that much.'

As the World's standard-setting racing driver, recognised

Above
Moss the Maestro was feared in the wet – here navigating Rob Walker's obsolete 4-cylinder Lotus 18/21, in the 1961 British GP.

globally as 'Mr Motor Racing', the transient World title paled into an irrelevance – lovely to win, but no greater proof of the man's truly transcendent quality.

Stirl had always been demanding of his teams. All truly professional racers are selfish; it goes with the territory. In period, perhaps, he redefined the term. When he had joined Aston Martin for sports car racing in 1956 their gentlemanly family ethos was suddenly shattered by a No 1 perfectly capable of trying every team car and then demanding one team-mate's, and insisting it should be fitted for him with the engine from another's. The same happened at Vanwall – 'first choice of equipment' was a feature of having Moss drive your cars. Often it paid off, other times his quest for some mechanical advantage did not.

After Vanwall bowed out at the end of 1958, Stirling arranged to drive Formula 1 cars – not for a factory team – but for the privateer Rob Walker, in rear-engined Cooper-Climax cars. Cooper would supply parts from which Rob's mechanics, led by Alf Francis, would build Stirl's cars, but Cooper could not help with a gearbox, so one was sourced instead from former Maserati transmission specialist Valerio Colotti. Stirling recalls: 'This Colotti gearbox would shoot us in the foot repeatedly, and we took a lot of stick for using it, but the truth of the matter is that we had no other choice.'

The Colotti 'box failed when he was leading the 1959 Monaco Grand Prix, and the Dutch. He drove a BRM prepared for him by the BRP team – run by 'Pa' and Ken Gregory – but second place at Aintree was his best result with it. Then back to the Walker Cooper for the German Grand Prix – where the Colotti 'box failed again – and then the Portuguese Grand Prix which it survived, and Stirling won: 'I was so pumped up with delight I couldn't sleep a wink that night!' He then won the Italian Grand Prix – two for the Cooper-Climax-Colotti – and the World title was again within his grasp into the final US Grand Prix at Sebring, Florida. But there his Colotti 'box lasted just six laps... before it broke again; another title lost.

By this time he was more philosophical. He was fully fledged as the yardstick against whom every other racing driver measured his performance. Through 1959 he had played a decisive role in Aston Martin becoming the first British marque ever to win the FIA Sports Car World Championship, and he had dominated Formula 2 in his Walker Cooper-Borgwards. Through 1960 his Walker Coopers were quickly replaced by the latest rear-engined Lotus 18, and he also drove sports Lotus 19s, the 'Birdcage' Maseratis, a Cooper Monaco, Formula 2 Porsche and a 3.8 Jaguar saloon.

But 1960 was punctuated by pain. Having won the Monaco GP first time out in Walker's new Lotus 18, he was practising at Spa for the Belgian GP when its left rear wheel came off. Stirl's diary entry for Saturday, June 18, 1960, reads bluntly: '*Shunt. Nose. Back. Legs. Bruises. Bugger!*' He had broken both legs and his nose and crushed three spinal vertebrae.

Very quickly he was walking again without sticks, then cycling around the hospital grounds. His surgeon Mr Urquhart even encouraged him to go dancing, checking out at 8pm and back at 1am. Stirl was well up for that – pulling birds had been his enthusiastic hobby since early teenage! 'I did all right,' he confirms. He was testing the Lotus 19 at Silverstone by July 25 and on August 7, a mere seven weeks after the Spa crash, he was racing again – winning in 'Pa' and Ken's new BRP Lotus 19 sports car at Karlskoga in Sweden.

Through 1961 the 'Sharknose' Ferraris dominated Formula 1 but for Stirl defeating them in the year-old Walker Lotus 18 at Monaco, and in the German GP at the Nürburgring – two of his greatest feats. He drove a Walker-entered Ferrari 250GT, shining at Le Mans and winning the Goodwood TT, for the fourth successive season. He also drove sports Porsches and into 1962 the Ferrari 'pre'-GTO, at Daytona.

Way back, in September 1951, Mr Ferrari had invited The Boy to drive his factory's latest 2½-litre 4-cylinder car in the Bari GP. He mentioned the possibility of Stirl then joining his works team for 1952. This was a year before he made the similar offer to Mike Hawthorn, which Mike accepted for '53. Stirl arrived at the Ferrari garage in Bari and sat himself in the Ferrari, only to have a mechanic demand what was he playing at? This wasn't his car, it was going to be driven by Piero Taruffi! Stirling was stunned; 'I was reduced to bumming around town to find an alternative drive, and was very grateful when David Murray offered me his old 2-litre V12 Ferrari instead. But it had the Continental foot pedal arrangement, with a centre throttle and right-side brake. I found it most confusing. Inevitably I hit the throttle pedal

Below
Typically calm concentration from Stirling at Brands Hatch, 1961, in the Cooper T53P Inter-Continental.

'I realised I had lost it; the automatic reflexes, the instinctive way of doing this, then that... I couldn't find it within me anymore'

when I meant to brake, and crashed it during first practice. Next day the engine blew and that was it. Ferrari had really dropped us in a hole. I did not forget, and I would not forgive, and because of that it always gave me great pleasure to beat those red cars – whenever I could.'

By 1961, Stirl had won two consecutive Goodwood TTs in the Ferrari 250GT, and his formerly distant relationship with Mr Ferrari improved. During the following winter they met at Maranello and *Il Drake* asked Moss to drive for him in 1962. 'But I wanted to continue driving for Rob, whose company and whose manner of going racing I really enjoyed. I told Mr Ferrari, "I would love to drive for you if the car is painted Walker blue, and you let Rob run it, while you supply and maintain it." We agreed in principle and I was also to drive a new 250GTO which was to be entered by my father and Ken Gregory's UDT-Laystall team.'

But it didn't happen. Driving one of Rob's Lotus 18/21s fitted with the new Climax V8 engine and run under UDT-Laystall colours, Stirl suffered his still unexplained accident at Goodwood on Easter Monday, 1962. The car collapsed under impact with the unyielding earth bank approaching St Mary's, crushing his face, breaking his nose, left arm and leg, squashing and tearing muscle and sinew, and bruising the right side of his brain so severely that he lay comatose for a

Above
At the 1959 TT with Lotus. From left, Alan Stacey, Colin Chapman, Mike Costin and Stirling.

month and was paralysed on his left side for a further six.

This ended his frontline professional career. On May Day, 1963, he drove a Lotus 19 again at Goodwood to judge his recovery. 'I realised – or rather thought I realised – that I had really lost it; the old automatic reflexes, the old instinctive way of doing this, then that. I couldn't find it within me any more. Despite being only 32, I confirmed my retirement.

'Looking back now, I appreciate my decision was premature. What I then believed to be permanent impairment was to a large extent only temporary. Subsequently, by the end of 1965, maybe mid-'66, I knew I was nearly mended properly. Sure, it would take some time to build up again, but I really felt I could do it. At 35 I was still young enough. But equally I had so many other business interests, life was so full of so many other things, that it simply wasn't possible to fit in a racing come-back.'

Wryly, friends suggested that in fact since Stirl had cashed the insurance pay-out, he was simply too mean to refund it! But we all celebrated the fact that he'd survived at all. He did return to racing, essentially for fun, but at least in part to prove that innermost belief to himself. A season with Audi in the 1980 British Saloon Car Championship showed him that racing had changed immensely in the years he'd been sidelined. Racing tactics and customs were light years away

Clockwise from left
With Graham Hill at Goodwood in 1962, just before Stirling's last ever race of his frontline career; visiting Walker Racing, post-accident and not long out of the coma; leaving hospital, June '62.

Above
Moss invented the profession of being a retired racing driver, which offered many benefits – as here with Carol Marshall, a Miss Universal Airport contestant, April 1970.

from those of his heyday. Not least, physical contact was becoming accepted, because with modern roll-over bars and belts and fire extinguishers payback was unlikely – the risks had been diminished, driving itself somehow devalued, the bar lowered, the golf hole enlarged. That disappointed him. It demeaned his sport. And so Historic racing beckoned, and Moss the Maestro has graced it for decades since. 'I'll keep on racing as long as I can enjoy it,' he says, 'I find the limit is much lower these days than it used to be, I'm past being brave, but I still love it Boy, I just love it.'

Domestically, he is a self-confessed baby snatcher, his third wife Susie having been his bubbly young PR lady around the time of that unloved Audi programme. But they have now enjoyed a fantastically close marriage for nearly 30 years, and form an absolutely inseparable team. In recent years Stirl's pain tolerance and recuperative powers have been tested repeatedly by the aftermath of his old racing injuries, especially in his spine, but after repeated surgery he remains the ever-active, dynamically bouncy ball he has always been. His motto 'Movement is tranquillity' is a lifestyle he still enacts to the extreme – as confirmed by the packed diary which Susie energetically maintains. He still loves telling silly jokes, and enjoys his own immensely. One of the latest is typical: 'Dustman can't find the wheelie bin at a house so he hammers on the door, and a Chinaman answers. "Mornin' mate," says the dustman, "where's yer bin?" Chinaman looks furtive then says, "I bin on toilet." Dustman realises he hasn't understood and says, "No mate, where's your wheelie bin?" And the Chinaman looks sheepish, then says, "Oh OK then – I wheelie bin 'avin' a w--k!" Stirl usually begins to giggle before he's reached the pay-off line, and can scarcely spluttter it out. Absolutely typical.

And for me a measure of Moss the Man was his comment when I first called to congratulate him on his long-overdue Knighthood. He said, 'you know Boy, what I'm really delighted about is that they've given me this gong in the same list as dear old Henry Cooper – a thoroughly good bloke!' Indeed, two really world-class British warriors together. But for me, it's quite straightforward. Here in 2009 Sir Stirling Moss is simply our greatest living Englishman. Bar none. △

MY TWO
PASSIONS

JOCHEN 70

THE MOSS
Family

Behind every successful man there tends to be a solid and supportive family. In the case of Sir Stirling, parents Alfred and Aileen along with sister Pat rallied to his cause while managing their own full and successful lives...
Words: Philip Porter

Above
When you are the proud father of a fantastic racing driver anxiety comes with the territory. Worried looks from Alfred, and first wife Katie, circa 1958.

A competitive nature and dogged determination are two traits that run through the Moss family: father Alfred, mother Aileen and sister Pat. So many of those who are ultra-successful have enjoyed the close support of their family in their younger, formative days and their first steps in the field they conquer. Stirling was no exception and, although his father was initially very much against his son having a go at motor racing, Alfred gave him his whole-hearted support. This extended beyond financial assistance, for Moss senior had been quite a useful driver himself and had competed at Indianapolis and Brooklands.

As a young boy Stirling enjoyed his junior school, but the same cannot be said for the rest of his education. 'I didn't enjoy senior school, which was 13-18, because I was teased, I was bullied – I suppose because I have got a Jewish name, although I am not Jewish. My Christian name is Scottish but that didn't make any difference.

'I enjoyed sport at school because I loved it. I was quite good at rugger and running, so I enjoyed that side, but the other aspects I didn't. Otherwise I did have a happy childhood. Up until the age of 16 my mother made me ride horses in show-jumping and gymkhana competitions, which I didn't particularly like. They are nice animals, but I didn't enjoy it much. Then my sister came along, who of course was really good, so that took the pressure off me. In principle, I had a very happy time when I was young. But, of course, the war was on.'

Germany invaded Poland about a fortnight before Stirling's 10th birthday, and Britain and its allies declared war, with the conflict lasting until the young Moss was 15. But living in the country, his life was not heavily impacted on by the escalating worldwide conflict.

'My father not only designed but patented a thing which became known as the Morrison Shelter for use during bombing raids. It really annoyed me because they named it after the politician Herbert Morrison. So we had these shelters over all our beds. We also did have a bomb

Below
Alfred Moss, February 1961: Moss senior designed and patented what later became the Morrison air raid shelter which was used extensively during the Second World War.

Above
Stirling and Alfred, 1948: while Moss senior was initially against Stirling going racing, Alfred supported his son wholeheartedly in his endeavours.

Above
Until Stirling turned 16 his mother made him ride horses – even though he didn't particularly enjoy the experience.

Left
Lake Garda, 1949: Stirling puts his best foot forward.

Above
August 30, 1959: Katie and Alfred Moss are seen in more relaxed mood at Brands Hatch.

shelter next door to the house. We didn't bother getting out of bed actually, because every night there was the bloody wailing of the air raid sirens.

'Of course we had to black out and all these things. That is the reason why the traffic lights now have a hood over them: it was for the war. They weren't there before the war. The military would send up barrage balloons and smoke. From a child's point of view it was quite exciting. You would hear a bloody doodlebug go over, which was bad. But as a kid you would go to the window, which you weren't supposed to do. The window would have tape on it so it wouldn't come in because of an explosion. Quite exciting for children. We were living then at Long White Cloud, which was Bray, Berkshire.'

Young Stirling avoided the worst of the Blitz but his father, who ran a host of dental practices in central London, did not. 'Dad had 15 or 16 surgeries that he would go round servicing. Invariably one would get bombed because they were all round London. You were not allowed to advertise as dentists in those days. So, if one of his practices got bombed he would go along with a caravan and put up signs: *Business as usual, A. Moss and Partners. Come in and have your teeth done!* He was terrible, my dad.'

The family were pretty close in the late 1940s and early 1950s, when Stirling made his first tentative steps into motor sport and Pat was starting to make a name for herself in the show-jumping arena. They were close but known for fighting each other. 'I would swear at my sister,' says Stirling, 'and she would swear back.'

Talking about those days before her sadly premature passing in 2008, Pat recalled that the family was very competitive among themselves. If they played cards or Scrabble, they would take it very seriously. The siblings did not get on so well until much later in life.

Stirling adds: 'The gap between you [in age] matters quite a lot in the early years. When you get older age doesn't come into it. Pat was a pain in the neck, with her horses and so on, when she was five or six – and because I was 11 or 12, we didn't really get on. Then she did very well jumping so therefore we didn't share that passion. We got along very well in the later years.'

After establishing herself as one of the top riders in the country and a member of the British team, Pat would go on to be the top women's rally driver in the world. With both sister and brother having busy, very separate careers, their paths would not cross that much, although

Above
Stirling and sister Pat. In their early years the siblings did not get on, but as time passed they grew closer.

Below
Pat Moss, Monaco, May 1961: Stirling's sister forged a great career in the rallying world.

'You would hear a doodlebug go over but as a kid you would go to the window'

Above
Basher circa 1946: a much-loved and valued member of the family.

Right
Despite Stirling's admission that show-jumping was not for him, it earned him vital prize money which went towards the first racer.

Stirling would go back to the family home, then in Tring, on Sundays whenever commitments allowed. He was very proud, though, to see Pat doing well on the international rallying scene.

'She did a terrific job because she had a very competitive nature; she was a pretty strong person. She had got a lot of stamina. She was very competitive, very determined. To win the Liège outright for a girl...' Pat not only won the Liège-Rome-Liège, considered to be the toughest rally in Europe, in a big Healey in 1961, but also finished second in the Alpine and RAC rallies that year. In 1962 she won the Tulip Rally outright, taking the first of many famous victories for a new phenomenon called the Mini. She won the European Ladies' Rally Championship five times.

It was that family determination which literally drove her on, the same determination her mother had shown in becoming the Ladies' Trials Champion of England, her father had demonstrated in building an empire in the world of dentistry and her brother had applied to become the greatest racing driver in the world. △

R-50-TN-AJ

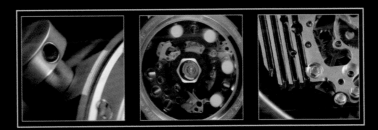

www.brm-manufacture.com

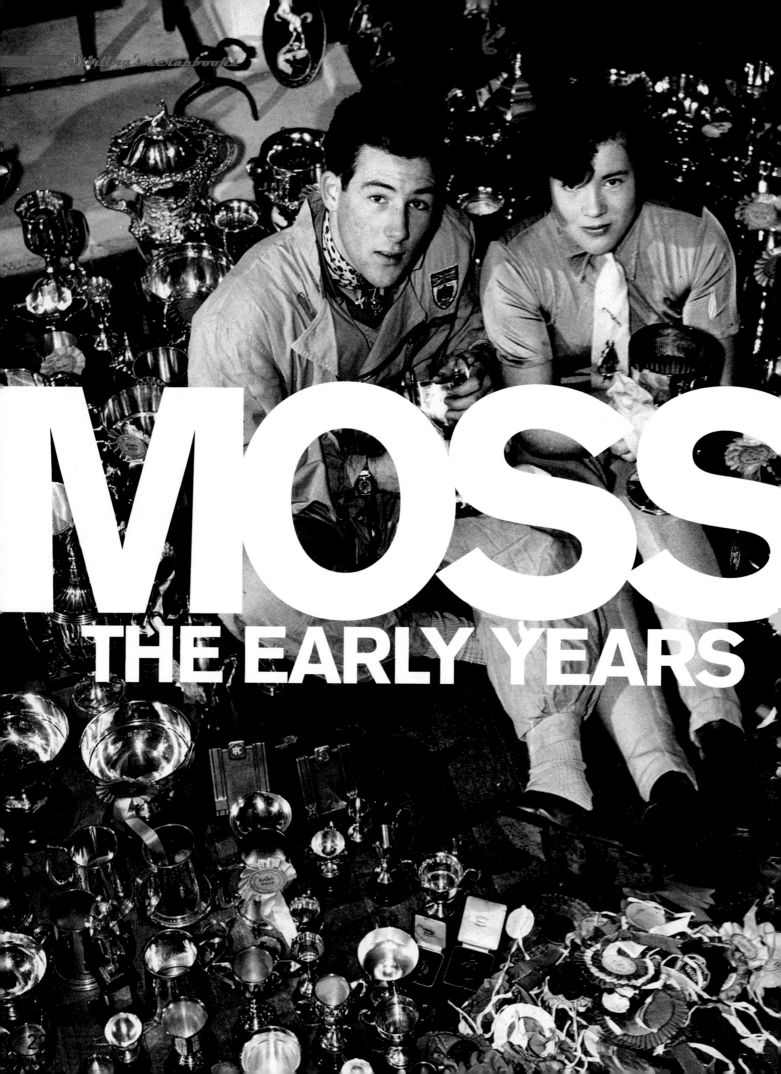

MOSS
THE EARLY YEARS

Taken from the series of acclaimed books based on the personal diaries and scrapbooks of Sir Stirling Moss, we sample the delights of his youth and early racing career...

Facing page
Stirling and his younger sister Patricia inherited their parents' competitive instincts: by 1948 they were both gathering trophies, Stirling for his motor racing and Pat for her horse riding.

When publisher Philip Porter suggested to Sir Stirling Moss that they might collaborate on some books based on the racer's old scrapbooks, Moss's reaction was: 'I think you're crazy, but OK.'

The first two volumes, which focused on two pivotal years in Moss's career – 1955 and 1961 respectively – were instant smash-hits. There then followed a third volume on Moss's boyhood and his first forays into racing, initially in the 500cc class and then with the big cars, starting with a Jaguar XK120 in the Dundrod TT. Abortive encounters with BRM and Ferrari, successful rallying in a Sunbeam-Talbot and the family purchase of a Maserati 250F are just some of the stories dealt with before Moss's end-of-1954 signing to drive for Mercedes-Benz.

Come with us now as we enjoy snippets from this fascinating book, which tells as much about the kind of man he was as the cars he drove... straight from the horse's mouth.

»

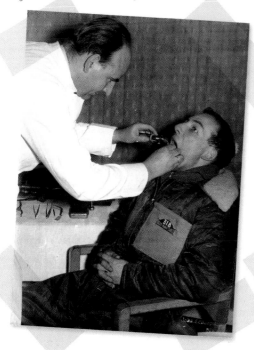

Left
Stirling's father, Alfred Moss, was also a motor enthusiast. In 1923 he went to Indiana, USA to study dentistry and successfully pretended that he was a famous European racing driver – which netted him a drive in the Indy 500 in a Frontenac-Ford. He finished 16th out of 22 starters.

Above
Aileen Moss, Stirling's mother, was also a very competitive driver, as this photo of her with an impressive array of trophies shows. She won the Ladies' Trials Championship in a 1.5-litre Singer and then moved up to a 2-litre Marendaz, with a supercharged Coventry Climax straight-six. Stirling remembers that it frequently blew up...

Right
Returning to England, Alfred set up in the garage business with his brother-in-law, Michael Lawson. Alfred seems to have picked up some American instincts for publicity: this shot shows him releasing homing pigeons during a call-out, which allegedly flew back to the garage with messages about what parts were needed!

'When Stirling was 18, he persuaded h

Right
Not much is known about this saucy siren, other than that she was called Marlene. Stirling always had an eye for the ladies and remembers being caught *in flagrante delicto* with his girlfriend Sylvia when he was 16 – by his mother!

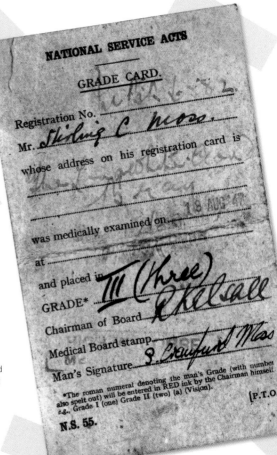

Left and right
Known as 'the Jeep', this stripped-down Austin Seven provided Stirling with his earliest motoring experiences in the grounds of the family's home. In 1947 he was excused National Service due to a kidney complaint (right): eight years later, when he was famous, questions were asked in Parliament about why he hadn't served, and he was forced to defend himself in public.

Repairs car in trailer, then wins climb

By OUR MOTORING CORRESPONDENT

ALTHOUGH a newcomer to motor racing and "baby" of the event, 18-year-old Sterling Moss, of Maidenhead, swept the board at the Prescott Hill climb near Cheltenham (Essex) yesterday by beating 14 veterans in the 500 c.c. class.

On Friday his Cooper Special car was not in a fit state to drive after a hill climb in Jersey.

Sterling, his father, mother and 13-year-old sister flew from Jersey to Southampton, picked up the car, put it in a trailer and dashed north to Prescott in the family saloon.

There was no time to stop for repair of the racing engine, so young Sterling and his mechanic rebuilt the engine in the trailer as the saloon raced north.

Right
When Stirling was a boy the family moved to a big house at Bray, Berkshire, with several acres of grounds and lots of animals. It's possible that, if Stirling hadn't become a racing driver, he might have gone into farming.

ther to buy him a new 500cc Cooper'   »

Right and above
Father and son at Silverstone's inaugural meeting in 1948, which hosted the first post-war British Grand Prix. Stirling was entered for the supporting 500cc race and set fastest time in practice; he was leading the race until a drive sprocket came loose. It's quite possible that the Brockbank cartoon, above, was inspired by Stirling's appearances at hillclimbs.

THIS MONTH'S COVER

Capturing public imagination is Stirling Moss as he goes from success to success with his Cooper 500 and 1000 c.c. Our cover shews him coming out for the start of Manx Cup Race. After putting up the fastest lap time of 67.78 m.p.h. he was forced out of the race ; but the biggest surprise he put up at this meeting was his practice lap of 72.35 m.p.h.

Left
For 1949, Stirling upgraded to a Cooper MkIII that could be fitted with either 500cc or 1000cc engines. At the age of 20 he finished third in the British Hillclimb Championship: he also started travelling abroad to race.

I TAKE OFF MY CAP TO MR. MOSS

John Heseltine, of Kingswood School, Bath, wins 10s. for this entry in "My Sports Hero Heroine" competition—because of his unusual choice.

FEW readers may know who Stirling Moss is and in what sport he competes. But he is my sports hero.

At 19 years of age Stirling Moss is himself servicing and racing a 500 c.c. racing car in competition road races and hill climbs. And he is winning.

The strength and stamina needed for handling a high performance racing car is as great as in any other sport.

I take my cap off to Stirling Moss!

Above
Everyday transport for Stirling was this sportily spatted Morris Minor – note the pillar-mounted spotlamp! As Stirling's racing career took off, his sister Pat was enjoying similar success in the world of show-jumping.

'Having been promised a car by Ferrari, h

Left and right
Stirling dances with Sally Weston, a regular part of his life during the early 1950s and the cause of much press speculation. Where women were concerned, however, even Stirling was out-charmed by Lance Macklin (right, with Stirling), who was older and, in Stirling's opinion, more sophisticated.

Left
After success with his Cooper and for John Heath's HWM team, Stirling got his big break in the 1950 Dundrod TT. Jaguar XK120 entrant Tommy Wisdom had secured a last-minute works drive for Jowett, so Stirling talked his way into the Jag. He won the race in very wet conditions, beating the two works XKs, and as a result William Lyons immediately asked him to head the Jaguar works team being created for 1951.

ACE 'LOST' HIS CAR

By Thomas Wisdom

BRITAIN'S 21 - year - old racing motorist, Stirling Moss, was yesterday robbed of a chance to drive a famous Grand Prix car.

The Italian racing-car chief, Enzo Ferrari, had invited him to drive a new car in yesterday's Bari Grand Prix.

Moss flew to Italy last week. But yesterday he saw an Italian, Piero Taruffi, drive the car into third place.

By telephone Moss said: "There seems to have been a misunderstanding. They say there would have been an outcry if an Italian had not driven the car."

Left
One car he didn't drive, however, was a Ferrari. Having been promised a car by Enzo Ferrari – at the time, Stirling was also being courted by BRM – for the Bari Grand Prix, he arrived in Italy to find that his car had been given to Piero Taruffi instead. The incident soured his attitude towards Ferrari forever.

...und it had been given to Taruffi instead'

»

Left
Stirling's manager, Ken Gregory, on left, seems to have adopted the popular New Elizabethan theme of 1952 for this New Year's Eve Ball – but is Stirling dressed as a Spaniard? And who knows what the lady next to him has come as...

Above and right
Both these cars were driven by Stirling at Boreham in August 1952, but whereas he had no trouble winning with the Jaguar, the G-type ERA – seen, right, being raced by Stirling at Zandvoort a few days later – was much harder work. He managed to come third in the ERA at Boreham but found the car unreliable and its Bristol engine not powerful enough against Ferraris.

Below
Resurfacing of the road being used for the 1953 Dundrod TT caused problems for the three C-types entered by Jaguar: 'It was as though the track was made of granite diamond cutters,' recalls Stirling. 'The maximum we managed on a set of tyres was seven laps.' All three C-types retired with gearbox failure, reputedly accelerated by wheels locking on the loose surface.

Charles Dunn.

News

Above and right
Stirling's trademark Patey helmet saved his life when he was punted into a roll-over by Tony Rolt's Connaught at Castle Combe: the helmet, seen being held by his sister Pat at his bedside during convalescence, right, was partially rubbed through by the track surface. As it was, he escaped with a broken right shoulder and a twisted knee.

STIRLING MOSS, Britain
ion racing motorist, in h
Bristol yesterday. At Castle
Wiltshire, on Saturday, his
lap was in a 50m.p.h. colli
Tony Rolt's Connaught. N
pitched on to the track as
overturned.
With his broken right sho
plaster and his arm in a sli
said that his only other injur
a twisted knee and some al
Later yesterday he left the h

B'ham Post 5-10-53

Stirling At Home
Ace racing motorist Stirling Moss, who crashed at Castle Combe, Wilts, on Saturday, is now recovering at his father's home in Tring. Here his sister Pat—famous as a show jumper—is at his bedside holding the crash helmet which probably saved his life.

Stirling Moss to drive for Mercedes

Above and below
The big news in December 1954 was that Stirling was signed by Mercedes; despite his innate patriotism, the lack of a comparable British team meant he had to look abroad. The diary extract from the previous January, below, reads: 'Cable from Ferrari with offer of drive. Spent all day to decide "no".'

AUTOSPORT, DECEMBER 3, 1954

749

Stirling Moss says:—

" *The more I race, the more I appreciate Ferodo Anti-Fade Brake Linings !*"

"When I'm racing, I naturally want t go as fast as I can for as long as I can— that's why I choose Ferodo Anti-Fade Brak Linings. When cornering for instance . . Ferodo Linings give me the confidence t keep my foot off the brake pedal till the ver last moment—and, as any lap chart shows seconds saved like that win races! And what' more, because Ferodo Linings can stand u to this scorching wear without fadin they stay efficient lap after lap!

Stirling Moss specifies
FERODO
ANTI-FADE Brake Linings

Jan 3rd To Tring + Bed 1 WAS worked a car all day Cable from Ferrari with offer of drive. Spent all day to decide "no". Bed 12 pm

Right
The Mercedes deal sealed Stirling's status as a 1950s superstar. One newspaper article estimated that he would be paid £20,000 a year by Mercedes, in addition to the money he earned from endorsements like this. He had come a long way in his six years as a racing driver...

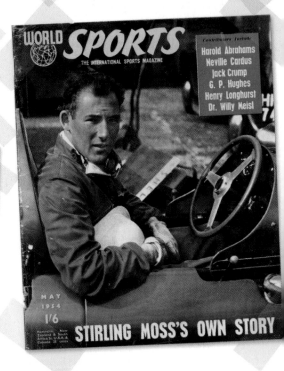

WORLD **SPORTS**
THE INTERNATIONAL SPORTS MAGAZINE

Contributors include:
Harold Abrahams
Neville Cardus
Jack Crump
G. P. Hughes
Henry Longhurst
Dr. Willy Meisl

MAY 1954 1/6
Australia, New Zealand & South Africa 2s. U.S.A. & Canada 25 cents

STIRLING MOSS'S OWN STORY

Stirling Moss Scrapbook 1929-1954

Pictures, cuttings and information in this feature are all taken from Stirling Moss Scrapbook 1929-1954. It is published by Porter Press International at £34.95, ISBN 978 0 9550068 8 3.

LAP OF
honour

Shortly before this Mercedes-Benz entered
retirement, we were invited to an exclusive last
outing in the most famous racing car in the world,
300SLR '722', with which Stirling Moss won the
1955 Mille Miglia in such legendary style
Words and photography: Mark Dixon

If you're a little bored with seeing this particular 300SLR, then we apologise. Yes, it was on the cover of issue 17 of our parent magazine *Octane* and it's appeared in the pages of that publication since then. But, in recent years, the life of '722' has been on the quiet side, as one of the stand-out exhibits at the Mercedes-Benz Museum in Stuttgart. Now it's much too valuable to be driven, believes the firm.

Forgive us, then, for indulging in this tribute to what is arguably the most famous racing car in the world. It is, after all, the 'signature' car of Stirling Moss, who drove it to victory in 1955 and who was its most regular pilot before its retirement from frontline PR service. Just before it went on static display in 2005, though, the offer from what was then DaimlerChrysler of a ride – and, who knows, maybe even a drive? – in 722 before it was mothballed, possibly forever, was too good to pass up.

On the final lap
Mercedes technician Gert Straub puts the pedal to the metal in 722, during one of its last outings before museum retirement.

Crunch time on the Targa
Moss had an 'off' during the 1955 Targa Florio, damaging 722's rad', but the car held together long enough for Moss and Collins to win.

Workmanlike office
Four-spoke wheel is detachable to allow driver access, but he then has to sit with legs splayed either side of the transmission tunnel.

One-two-three at Eifelrennen
In fact, SLRs nos 1, 2 and 3 finished one-two-four at the Eifelrennen in May 1955: here Kling leads Fangio, who finished first, and Moss.

'The twin exhausts that exit halfway along the offside are irresistibly reminiscent of gun barrels'

Moss says he can remember the precise moment at which he was won over to join the Mercedes team for 1955. 'I went for a try-out in the middle of winter – it was Hockenheim – and I drove this new W196 Formula One car, and because it had inboard brakes you got dust on your face. I used to wear large goggles and so I had a "panda face", with white eyes and black face. I got out of the car and was looking around for a bit of rag. Up comes a mechanic, clicks his heels, bends forward – there's a bowl of water in his hands, but not just a bowl of water, it's hot water – as well as a piece of soap, and over his arm is a towel. And I thought, my God, this is something.'

The car that Moss had been sampling that winter's day at Hockenheim was the W196: the open-wheeled, Grand Prix version of what would become the 300SLR. Juan Manuel Fangio won two World Championships for Mercedes in 1954 and 1955, driving the W196 F1 car, but it was Moss who dominated with the sports-racer 300SLR in 1955. Besides the Mille Miglia, which he won at an all-time-record average speed of 97.960mph (157.651kph), Moss also came first in the Dundrod TT (with John Fitch) and the Targa Florio, co-driven by Peter Collins. On both occasions he beat Fangio into second place.

But it's for the Mille Miglia that Moss and his SLR will always be remembered. Few people know that Moss' SLR is chassis number 0004; everyone recognises its Mille Miglia race number of 722, signwritten in bold Roman numerals like the identity of a Tiger tank. The impressively large number simply signifies that Moss and co-driver Denis Jenkinson were due to start from Brescia at 7.22am on May 2, 1955.

Facing page
Rare glimpses of 722's spaceframe chassis, snapped during a stripdown prior to it taking part in the 2005 Mille.

The start number is not the only militaristic feature of Moss' SLR. The silver-painted, aerodynamic body recalls the bare-alloy and silver-doped fighter-aircraft prototypes of the early 1930s, and the twin exhausts that exit halfway along the offside are irresistibly reminiscent of gun barrels. But the greatest similarity with aircraft is in the engineering. Mercedes capitalised on its wartime aero-engine experience by equipping the 300SLR with direct mechanical injection into each cylinder.

The SLR engine is a marvellous thing. Not a beautiful one, draped as it is in an *Alien*-like cradle of pipes and hoses, but technically ingenious and superbly made. Like a pre-war Bugatti straight-eight, it has two four-cylinder integral heads and blocks mounted on a common crankcase, with a built-up crankshaft running in roller bearings. The crankcase is made of aluminium alloy, the blocks of Silumin alloy, and the valves are both opened and closed mechanically by twin camshafts.

More remarkably, drive to the clutch is via a shaft running from the mid-point of the engine, and the propshaft then passes between the driver's legs en route to the rear transaxle. The clutch pedal is therefore a good 24 inches to the left of the brake and accelerator, which are crowded together on the right of the transmission tunnel. This causes some involuntary amusement when, the first time I come to brake, my enormous size 13 right foot depresses both brake and throttle simultaneously. My, how the Mercedes people laughed, as their impossibly valuable piece of history disappeared towards the horizon...

Tempting as it is to describe how I thrashed 722 around the Mercedes test track, stirring memories of a youthful Moss and causing elderly Neubauer-lookalikes to tip their Homburgs in tearful homage, the truth is that no outsider below the rank of F1 pilot is allowed to drive 722 in anger these days. My own experience was limited to a few low-gear trundles up and down the infield.

But workshop manager Gert Straub is one of the hallowed few permitted to let 722 off the leash, and Denis Jenkinson's seat beckons. Privilege though it is, I'm secretly thankful we won't be doing more than a few laps of the test track, because Jenks' narrow bucket seat – trimmed, like Moss', in kitsch 1950s checked cloth – would be more at home in a pedal car.

Push in the ignition key to activate the fuel pumps, turn the mag' switch on, and press the starter. The engine's fuel-injected, of course, so it ignites immediately. ❯❯

'Sitting aft of the engine is like standing alongside a Messerschmitt 109 as the pilot warms up the oil'

My God, it's noisy! Fantastic, thrilling, exhilarating, but so noisy! Sitting aft of the engine is like standing alongside a Messerschmitt 109 as the pilot warms up the oil. Raw, mechanical, shrieking – it's all those things, but most of all it's just bloody loud.

From my shopping-trolley manoeuvres I know that the clutch is sharp-ish but not too heavy, and that the gear lever moves with the solid, mechanical feel you'd expect of a 1950s Mercedes. The polished gate is a work of art, with a tactile little lock-out lever to prevent you selecting reverse by mistake. You also have to depress a button on top of the gearknob in order to move into the first-reverse slot.

Now, Gert Straub takes his responsibilities seriously, and that means ensuring 722 is ready for the kind of no-nonsense treatment that Moss and, on the 2005 Mille retrospective the car is destined for at time of writing, Jochen Mass are likely to dish out. The car is already thoroughly warmed, so he just points that long silver nose out of the pitlane, and floors it.

Jeeeeeez! This car is not just as loud as an Me109, it accelerates like one, too. With a power-to-weight ratio similar to that of a Lamborghini Countach, it just squats on its haunches and goes – whatever speed you're doing. And it'll keep on going to nearly 180mph, for as long as the driver can handle it: on the long, straight sections of the '55 Mille, Moss regularly saw over 170mph with the engine nudging its 7500rpm red line.

Opposite page
Riding the banking on Mercedes' factory test track, 50 years after Moss and Jenkinson's epic win on the 1955 Mille Miglia.

Noise level apart, 722 is a reasonably comfortable machine in which to burn up the kilometres. Inboard-mounted drum brakes help keep the unsprung weight down, which benefits the ride – although they were also responsible for those 'panda faces' mentioned by Moss, since the brake dust is sucked straight through the cockpit. Disc brakes would have been more effective but drums did the job, even when the friction material had worn away and the aluminium backing plates were hard against the drums' inner faces, as they were by the end of the '55 Mille. Moss remembers that their biggest drawback was a habit of locking on when the linings crazed: Mercedes' solution (but not on 722) was to install buttons in the cockpit, one for each front wheel, to inject a drop of oil into the affected drum at crucial moments.

Those inboard brakes probably help explain why the SLR's steering is remarkably light, even at walking pace. I can personally vouch for that, if not for the fact that it is also superbly precise at race speeds. Hanging the gearbox at the back of the car gives a front/rear weight distribution of about 42/58 percent, and the low centre of gravity means that the rear wheels' single-pivot swing axle rarely causes anxiety unless the driver is exceptionally careless. Nevertheless, when spectators on the Mille Miglia occasionally threatened to block Moss' path, he would deploy the novel technique of wiggling the steering wheel violently so that it looked as though he was losing control; sometimes this encouraged the crowd to pull back – '…but not always'.

Inevitably, there were times when even Moss was caught out. Four times on the Mille Miglia, in fact. On the Dundrod TT, a rear-wheel blow-out ripped the magnesium-alloy body apart but, again, the damage wasn't enough to prevent Moss' car finishing, and winning. And on the Targa Florio in October 1955, Moss left the road, skidded down a slope and ended up in a field. The Mercedes mechanics patched up 0004's damaged radiator and Moss' co-driver Peter Collins rejoined the race – adding a few more scars on 0004's bodywork along the way. Needless to say, the Moss/Collins partnership won the event, 'despite all the efforts of Stirling and me to smash the car up,' as Collins said later. Such heroic exploits, of course, simply add to the magic.

Despite its eventful competition career, 722 is believed to be remarkably original, even down to its spaceframe chassis. As time passes, that originality becomes increasingly precious, which is one reason why 722 is now mothballed and its PR duties passed on to sister car 658, Fangio's mount on the 1955 Mille Miglia.

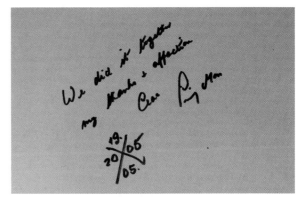

Stirling's signature
The bodywork has been signed by Moss himself: 'We did it together – my thanks and affection. Ciao, Stirling Moss.'

Double jeopardy
To prevent accidental changes into first or reverse gears, first is protected by a button in the gearknob, and reverse by a lock-out.

Ultimate head restraint
Most SLRs needed only a single cockpit fairing – for the driver – but another was provided for Jenkinson on the 1955 Mille Miglia.

Lightweight shell
722's bodyshell is constructed of magnesium alloy, rather than aluminium; what would happen in a fire doesn't bear thinking about.

Mercedes-Benz 300SLR

SPECIFICATIONS

Engine
2982cc straight-eight, alloy crankcase and blocks, desmodromic overhead valves, direct fuel injection

Power
310bhp @ 7500rpm

Transmission
Five-speed manual, rear-wheel drive

Suspension
Independent via torsion bars, single-pivot swing axle at rear, hydraulic dampers

Brakes
Inboard-mounted drums

Weight
880kg (1940lb)

Performance
0-60mph 7sec (est)
Top speed 180mph

'The engine is a marvellous thing. Not a beautiful one, but technically ingenious and superbly made'

'To be honest, I feel that 722 has been over-exposed in recent years,' said DaimlerChrysler Classic's manager Josef Ernst shortly before 722 was tucked away in its safe museum environment in Stuttgart. 'In future, it will be used much more sparingly. I'm not saying that it will never come out of the museum again – but the way the cars are to be displayed means that moving it will not be so easy as it is in the present location.'

The journalists, racing drivers and assorted hangers-on who have inveigled themselves into the hot seat of 722 in the past can therefore count themselves extremely fortunate. As do I, even if my experience lasted more like 1000 yards than 1000 miles. But hey, a drive is a drive, right? I've still tucked myself behind the steering wheel of what is probably the world's most famous racing car and been able to make it go, albeit briefly, and that's something to tell the grandchildren – if I ever have any. △

The Stuttgart home of '722'

On May 19, 2006, the new Mercedes heritage museum opened in Stuttgart-Untertürkheim, superseding the existing and cramped facility that had housed the company's historic exhibits within the Mercedes works complex.

The distinctive and striking building is shaped like a 'curved triangle' and features a continuous internal ramp, alongside which hundreds of vehicles from Mercedes' massive collection are displayed. Visitors can ride to the top of the 47m-high museum in lifts and then make a leisurely descent to the ground floor, with state-of-the-art media and communication systems to entertain them.

The huge scale allows Mercedes to showcase about 40 of its race and record-breaking cars, including 300SLR '722'. Historic commercial vehicles also share in the limelight.

A new centre for the sale of modern Mercedes is alongside, but the two buildings are run as completely separate operations.

Lounge Chair & Ottoman
Design: Charles & Ray Eames, 1956

Designed to last for generations.
Since 1956 the Eames Lounge Chair has been
the modern icon of luxury and comfort.

vitra.
The Authorised Original

RETURN
OF
THE
Gullwing

When Stirling Moss was preparing for the 1955 Mille Miglia, this is the car he used. Now, after 30 years hidden away, it's back in circulation
Words: Robert Coucher Studio photography: LAT

Even though times may be tough at the moment, it is still hard to imagine how bleak Western Europe was in the early 1950s. The continent was largely broken and Britain was just ending a decade of post-war rationing with the arrival of that outrageously exotic fruit, the banana…

With help from the Marshall Plan, Germany had been effectively rebuilding its heavy engineering industries after World War Two, and Mercedes-Benz was one of the manufacturers which moved quickly to re-establish its pre-eminence. Against the wishes of pre-war Mercedes-Benz racing chief, Alfred Neubauer (who had achieved success before the conflict with purpose-built racing cars), chief designer Rudolf Uhlenhaut persuaded the board that a stop-gap racing car would restore Mercedes' honour. The 300SL he came up with did just that; by winning at Le Mans in 1952.

Although America had paid dearly in lives lost in WW2, its economy was strong and many returning soldiers had picked up the desire for European automobiles. Maximilian Hoffman, who was responsible for importing many European sports cars to America, saw the racing 300SL and placed an order for 1000 roadgoing versions; the 300SL was first seen at the New York International Motor Sports Show in February 1954. It soon became known as the Gullwing.

The Gullwing you see here, chassis number 1980404500019, the 19th 300SL constructed, was shown at the Paris Salon Mondiale de l'Automobile in September 1954. It then became the Mercedes-Benz (Great Britain) press car and featured in *The Autocar* road test in 1955. It was also the 300SL used by Stirling Moss prior to his assault on the 1955 Mille Miglia, one of his most famous and emphatic victories for Mercedes-Benz. As Stirling says, 'PLB 23 features in my book, *Stirling Moss Scrapbook 1955*, where I was photographed driving the car during the preparation period for my Mille Miglia victory in 1955. I am delighted that PLB 23 has survived in such fine form and hope that it finds the proud and caring ownership that its long and uniquely important history deserves.'

In his book, he notes that he 'would spend a good deal of time in April practising for the Mille Miglia and would use the 300SL for much of it.' Photographs also show Moss driving the Gullwing at Brands Hatch in heavy snow in February of that year.

PLB 23

Of course, Moss and Jenks won the 1955 Mille Miglia driving a fearsome eight-cylinder Mercedes-Benz SLR in a record average speed of 97.93mph, but it is true to say that the roadgoing Gullwing had been a direct development of Uhlenhaut's 300SL racer of 1951. While Mercedes-Benz was on the up again by 1950, it did not have the sort of budget available for another full Grand Prix operation of the sort Alfred Neubauer had conducted in the 1930s. Chief engineer Fritz Nallinger suggested the development of a sports racing car using the 300 engine in 1951, so Neubauer and team drivers Hermann Lang and Karl Kling went to that year's Le Mans to have a look at the opposition.

They returned to Stuttgart with their work cut out. They had to best the Jaguar C-type's 220bhp and challenge Ferrari's 4.1-litre V12 grunt. With a projected 170bhp from the Mercedes-Benz 300 engine, low weight was crucial and the engineers set about developing the SL's lightweight tubular frame, which came in at just 70kg. The manner in which the tubes ran down the sides of the cars to provide torsional stiffness meant that regular doors were not possible so the engineers came up with the striking Gullwing arrangement. The competition cars (only 29 in total) were clad in aluminium but the roadgoing models were constructed of steel with aluminium doors, bonnet and boot lid. They weighed some 80kg more.

The saloon's engine was massaged and improved, and fitted with mechanical fuel injection – a first for a roadgoing car. Power was tweaked up to 215bhp for the normal engine with 8.55:1 compression ratio, and 225bhp for the 9.5:1 high-compression version. No fewer than five different rear axle ratios were offered to suit owners' preferences, for either storming up Alpine passes or for flat-out autobahn work.

In total just 1440 Gullwings were sold between 1954 and 1957 and all were bought by well-heeled drivers. And you did have to be extremely well-heeled to own one. In 1955 the British list price for a 300SL, including taxes, was £4392. A lot

'I was photographed driving the car during the preparation period for my Mille Miglia victory in 1955 – I'm delighted that PLB 23 has survived'

Clockwise from above
Recommissioned after 30 years in storage; Moss demonstrates the car at Brands Hatch; testing in the snow, again at Brands Hatch.

of money when a Ford Zephyr Six cost £754, a Jaguar D-type was £2685 and an Aston Martin DB3S was listed at £3684!

By 1955 Stirling Moss was established as one of the best racing drivers of the day. Here was a star who Mercedes-Benz was keen to have drive its special road cars, and PLB 23 was very much available to him. This car was also subjected to a full road test by *The Autocar* in which it received a glowing review.

Not surprising. In 1955 it was the McLaren F1 of its day. The car was fitted with the standard 3.64:1 rear axle ratio, making it docile in traffic. But when the revs breached 3500rpm the driver 'feels he is being rocketed through space,' even though the engine note was 'somewhat harsh at 6000rpm.' The car was timed at 135mph in poor conditions, with the 0-60mph dash taking 8.8 seconds. The finned drum brakes were powerful and suffered no fade – even though Jaguar had proved that discs were by then better – but the clutch was found to be rather heavy.

The Gullwing did suffer one hindrance; the rear suspension. While the front end was taken care of by double wishbones, coil springs, dampers and an anti-roll bar, the rear end relied on the proprietary Mercedes swing axle, which could lead to oversteer in extremis. *The Autocar* was not so impolite as to actually criticise the 300SL's handling but it did state 'humpback bridge signs should be treated with real respect,' and that 'any inclination to ease the throttle (when cornering) and the rear of the car will tend to swing around.' A bit of a handful then.

To be fair, PLB 23 was tested in winter and it was shod with 'racing pattern tyres, and their sound rose to a not unpleasant crescendo as the speed went up.' Now

'In 1955 the list price for a 300SL was £4392. A lot of money when a Ford Zephyr cost £754, a Jaguar D-Type was £2685 and an Aston DB3S was £3684'

Gullwings wear much more effective rubber and those on fast road events seem to be set low, with visible negative camber at the rear to help counter the effects of these swing axles.

Today PBL 23 looks remarkably original and straight. The car shows just 56,000 miles on the clock and it has not, thank God, been painted West Coast red. It has apparently been resprayed once and the original seats were at some stage recovered in leather, but these have since been returned to the original Mercedes-Benz tartan weave so redolent of the period. With its white-rimmed steering wheel, side engine vents, bolt-on eyebrows over the wheelarches and deliciously curvaceous shape, it is no wonder the Gullwing is such a desirable car. And PLB 23's history adds to its special allure.

Mercedes-Benz (Great Britain) sold PLB 23 to HWM in July 1956. In September 1956 HWM sold the car to racing driver Peter Woozley, who finished second in the Stanley Sears Trophy race at Snetterton in 1959 and set the fastest lap in a Mercedes 300SL, believed to be PLB 23. He then sold the car to Claude Walsingham of Walsingham Garage, who sold it to Melvyn Farrar in 1976. It then went into storage and disappeared from view for over three decades. Recently unearthed, this Gullwing, with its continuous history including signed documentation from Sir Stirling Moss, has now been sympathetically recommissioned and is ready for fast touring in the style it deserves.

Thanks to Cars International Kensington Limited, www.carsinternational.com. The *Stirling Moss Scrapbook 1955* **is available from www. porterpress.co.uk at £34.95.**

'This car was subjected to a full road test by *The Autocar*, in which it received a glowing review'

THE *Art* OF DRIVING

Seeing Stirling Moss drive competitively is like watching a genius create a masterpiece. Here, the artist himself reveals some of his secrets
Words and pictures: Philip Porter

PP: 'Driving fast obviously consists of many factors including reading the road, braking, setting up the car, steering, balancing on the throttle, getting the power down, different lines, experimenting...'

SM: 'A lot of that is gained purely by experience. When I first drove, I knew nothing at all about how cars handled. Then I did quite a lot of work with Alf [Francis, chief mechanic at HWM]. He said, "Well, let's try these different shock absorbers". So I got to know a lot about practical things: if you do this, that is likely to happen...

'We also had a lot of testing to do on tyres and stuff like that, which gave me quite a lot of mileage. The races were much longer, remember, three hours or so. So my amount of racing mileage – I have never even tried to calculate it at all, but I must have done a enormous amount of miles, 100,000 or something like that in a racing car – under racing conditions ≫

Below
Following his great friend and mentor Juan Manuel Fangio in Mercedes W196s at the 1955 British Grand Prix.

Above
'The earlier you can get onto the throttle the better, providing you are not taking corrective action, because that slows you down a lot. People don't realise that once you start correcting, it is knocking the speed off very quickly.'

means a lot of experience. You learn what cars will do. Cars have characteristics, understeer or oversteer, and in between. They all have their different foibles. Even two, so-called identical cars are different.

'One's style of driving for the Mille Miglia is quite different to the style of driving for Monaco. At Monaco, when you are going into a corner, you work out where your apex is and drive it accordingly. When you are on an open road, you can't. You don't know where the apex is, the Mille particularly, because you have got a lot of people lining the sides of the road and they obscure it. Therefore you have to drive in a different style, so you go in as near ten-tenths as you can and if something is wrong you then apply extra steering and back off sharply, so you then put on full opposite lock just to drop the speed. Drop the speed as soon as you can by any manoeuvre. That is quite a different style.

'I think hillclimbs are the best place to start because the only person you are driving against is yourself. You are testing your own natural ability. When you have gone up and you try something, it shows you fairly graphically; yes that worked or it didn't. In racing, of course, you keep going into a corner and you try one line then you may try a slightly different entrance and so on until you find the best one.

'The way to tell how quickly you are coming into a corner is to take a reading on your rev counter as you leave the corner, rather than any other way, I find. At Goodwood, for instance, as I leave the double right-hander after the start, I want to be getting 4600 or whatever it is. You try yourself out and against other people. When there are other people there and they brake you know, really and truly, that if you can't brake later than them, then you need to do something else. I think it took me many years to learn how to brake really late.

It's a very difficult manoeuvre and very destabilising to the car as well.

'The point is, what you have got to try and do is get onto the brake as late as you can and bring the throttle in as early as you can. Getting on the throttle earlier is more important than braking later but you have got to try and get the two together. The earlier you can get onto the throttle the better, providing you are not taking corrective action, because that slows you down a lot. People don't realise that once you start correcting, it is knocking the speed off very quickly.

'A four-wheel drift really should be classified as having the wheels all in the same line. If the front wheels are turned at all, it has actually got correction on; it isn't therefore a proper four-wheel drift.'

PP: 'Is what you call a proper four-wheel drift the quickest way through a corner?'
SM: 'I reckon it is. Providing you are starting on the outside of the track, touching the apex and going to the outside, and having to do that. I reckon you want to use all the road you possibly can but a lot of people don't.'

PP: 'And have it pointing straight as you exit the bend?'
SM: 'Oh yes. If you have to use correction to do that, then obviously you have slowed yourself down. You would probably be quicker the next lap to go a little bit slower and hold it in there.'

PP: 'Would you describe motor racing as a team sport or not? Obviously, you can't do without the mechanics and the support of the designers and that sort of thing but when you were out there you were pretty much on your own.'

'I pushed myself as hard as I possibly could once at the Nürburgring and I was absolutely wrecked for at least a week'

Clockwise from above
Hard cornering being demonstrated at the 1959 Oulton Park Gold Cup; more rapid progress at Brands Hatch the same year; a picture of steely concentration in Nassau.

SM: 'It is only a team sport when you are running two drivers with a car, which, of course, I have done and I enjoy. I wouldn't really call it a team sport. You are very much on your own, aren't you?'

PP: 'And that appeals to you? You wouldn't want to be in a team sport?'
SM: 'Yes, I would say that. I can blame myself, I can beat myself harder, I can force myself to do things. There are things that I have done or made myself do which would not be realistic or right for me to try and do to somebody else; it would be quite wrong. It is a personal thing.'

PP: 'Did you take risks?'
SM: 'Calculated risks, yes. The thing is, it is really quite hard work being in a car and driving flat out. I pushed myself as hard as I possibly could, I remember once, at the Nürburgring. I had done 40 laps out of 44, or something, and I was absolutely wrecked for at least a week. In the Alpine, I remember I drove terribly hard in one particular section because I had to and got into the control in time; the upside is so worthwhile that I wouldn't mind doing it. Being on one's own, you are where the buck stops; you can make all the decisions and that is what I like. I don't think it is right that I should be able to push really dangerous things onto other people. To risk my neck is one thing but I don't think it is right if I risk yours as well.'

PP: 'How important was winning? Would you have risked your neck?'
SM: 'Bloody important, yes. I suppose it is a surfeit of ego or pride, really. It gave me a tremendous amount. Certainly

being faster than the other people in the team; that is what mattered.'

PP: 'Would you frighten yourself sometimes?'
SM: 'I wouldn't normally frighten myself. There are times when I would be frightened by what happened. The most fear that I had in racing was before the flag fell. Once the flag falls, then I am not worried about it. I was really worried about the Mille Miglia because I didn't know the circuit. Once the flag went down, I had got a job to do and that was it, that takes over. If you go round a corner and it was a bit too quick and you damn nearly buy it, that is when you know the risk you have taken.'

PP: 'Would you always have a little margin?'
SM: 'I always used to endeavour to leave myself a small margin, yes I did. I think poor old Stuart Lewis-Evans probably didn't. He was very fast, really fast. I always tried to drive within my capabilities, yes.'

PP: 'Were there drivers who worried you because you felt they were about to have an accident?'
SM: 'There were drivers that you would know to keep away from, chaps like Willy Mairesse. You wouldn't go too close.'

PP: 'They were taking chances or wild?'
SM: 'Wild. If a guy was really good, then it was a different situation. You could follow him closely, like I followed Fangio in 1955. I had great confidence in his abilities.'

PP: 'Why do you think you were better than other people?'
SM: 'Determination, stamina. I think that I could understand

the language of the car, because all cars will give you a warning of one thing or another, I reckon I could interpret that earlier and more effectively that many others might have been able to.'

PP: 'You must have had supreme reactions?'
SM: 'My reactions were very fast. I know that because they were tested. People always say that reactions are what really matter and I did have fast reactions but they, I think, are things that make you a bit safer. What makes you even safer than fast reactions is doing the right thing. However quick you are, if you do the wrong thing, it is no bloody good. You use reactions to get you out of trouble, not get you into it. If they are misused, for example if you over-correct, then you are starting to fish-tail.'

PP: 'But that is skill and experience; you get used to that. Balance must have been fundamental?'
SM: 'Yes.'

PP: 'Holding a car, steering on the throttle...'
SM: 'The point is that you have to learn that to steer a car, you have got a steering wheel, but that isn't the only way to steer it. A wheel, to my mind, is used to just start the car pointing in the right direction. It says, I am going to go right, I am going to go left. After that you use it to compensate. So, if you

are going into a corner and you want more steering, you apply more power. It is a case of balancing that when you are going into a corner. It is a case of understanding the dynamics and the balance of the car. To my mind, that comes from the experience of driving.'

PP: 'You have said that you were racing so often that it became almost second nature. You were driving more than probably anyone else.'
SM: 'Exactly, it is very important. To brake really late in my mind is what makes drivers such as Lewis Hamilton so exciting. He is a very good braker and, if you brake late, it gives you an opportunity to pass people without having to outcorner them. That is quite important because you can't effectively pass a semi-comparable driver going round a corner. That just can't happen. If he is not much bloody good, then you can.

'Getting in the rhythm is so important. If you can go to the Nürburgring and get in the rhythm and feel it, you can get quicker and quicker without necessarily having to make more demands. It is an amazing thing. When you get into the rhythm of a car, it makes an enormous difference. I can understand getting in the rhythm around the Nürburgring, I find it very difficult to understand getting in the rhythm of the Mille Miglia but somehow I must have managed to do it because it flowed so nicely.' △

Above
'You've got a steering wheel but that isn't the only way to steer a car. A steering wheel, in my mind, is used to just start the car pointing in the right direction. After that you use it to compensate.'

Maserati
250F

**In May 1956 Stirling Moss drove to victory
in the 14th Monaco Grand Prix, behind the
wheel of this 250F. His win was the first for
a British driver, in Monte Carlo, since 1929
– and hard-fought it certainly was...**
Words: David Burgess-Wise
Photography: Michel Zumbrunn

When the grand prix circus came to town for the 14th Monaco GP in mid-May 1956, Monte Carlo was still very much in a state of euphoria following the fairytale wedding of Prince Rainier and 27-year-old Hollywood star Grace Kelly. With Mercedes out of competition after the traumas and triumphs of the 1955 season, Stirling Moss had returned to Maserati, but this time as lead driver of the works team rather than as the privateer he had been before he signed for Mercedes. 'It was like going back to an old friend,' he recalls. 'The 250F is a car that was always very user-friendly and well suited to Monaco, which is quite a tricky circuit.'

His team mates were the previous year's lead driver Jean Behra, a tough little Frenchman whose prosthetic ear was the consequence of a bad crash in the 1955 Ulster TT, and a young hopeful from Bologna named Cesare Perdisa.

Because of the tight, twisting nature of the Monaco circuit, the race organisers had fixed a starting limit of 16 cars, to be selected from the 18 entries – mostly works teams – on the basis of practice times. As an extra incentive there was a prize of £100 for the driver making the fastest practice lap on the first day. And if that seems like peanuts today, 50 years ago it

represented several months' wages to the average worker (and quite a bit to the average racing driver, too).

One of the most handsome racing cars of that charismatic era, the 250F Maserati had made its first appearance in 1954, its 2.5-litre six-cylinder engine a bored-out development of the 2-litre unit that Maserati had raced in the Formula Two series that had ended in 1953. Its block and crankcase were a single casting of light alloy with pressed-in dry liners, and the accuracy of Maserati's machining was ably demonstrated by it not having a single gasket anywhere in the engine. Circular rubber seals seating in grooves machined in the joint face kept the water out of the cylinders, with other joints being made by closing metal to metal with jointing compound.

The seven-bearing crankshaft ran in Vandervell thin-wall lead-bronze bearings. It had two balance weights to each throw, but not the characteristic vibration damper seen on six-cylinder engines since Edwardian days, when 'power rattle' had plagued the undamped pioneering sixes made by companies such as Napier.

So that a larger inlet valve could be used, the classic twin-cam head had two valves per cylinder set at unequal angles; the camshafts were driven by a train of gears at the front of the engine which also drove an auxiliary shaft operating twin

Below
Sir Stirling Moss remembers the 250F as a 'user-friendly' car that was ideal for the Monaco circuit.

Marelli magnetos, one feeding a spark plug at the front of each cylinder, the other a plug at the rear of the cylinder. While this minimised the risk of ignition failure, it did demand meticulous setting up.

Standard carburation involved three twin-choke Webers, although Stirling had some success with fuel injection on his own Maserati; for 1956 the factory had fitted some engines with carburettors and some with an experimental mechanical fuel-injection system, designed by Maserati, that used slide throttles like a racing Amal carburettor. It worked satisfactorily, though whether it actually improved on the carburettors was debatable.

Stirling, offered the choice between carburettors and fuel injection, went for the Webers, though he practised with both types: 'I chose the carburettors because the response was better than the injection set-up, which wasn't fully sorted.'

Again, given the option of a four-speed transmission or the later five-speed transaxle, Stirling chose the configuration that would best exploit the bottom-end torque characteristics of the engine: 'I opted for the four-speed box, much to Maserati's surprise, because it gave me less opportunity to change gear. Although they were very proud of their five-speed you didn't need it on a circuit like Monaco, where the

maximum speed was only about 125mph.'

The rear-end set-up was classic de Dion, with the dead axle sprung on a transverse leaf spring; front suspension was coil and wishbone. The main fuel tank was immediately behind the driver, with the extreme tail of the car housing a large oil tank for the engine's dry-sump lubrication system.

As is well known, Stirling doesn't like driving cars with centre throttle pedals, and Maserati had gone out of their way to satisfy him by equipping the three models set aside for him with right-hand pedals.

The Maserati service garage was about halfway round the circuit, on the downhill section between the station and the sea, so that the drivers could change cars at the midpoint of a lap, during practice. During the first practice session on May 10, the Thursday before the race, Stirling lapped his carburettor-equipped car in 1min 46.2sec to better the fastest time of the ameliorato Lancia-Ferrari driven by his former

Below
Lengthy tail of 250F houses main fuel tank and a large oil reservoir for the dry-sump engine.

'The Maserati garage was about halfway round the circuit, between the station and the sea, so that the drivers could change cars at the midpoint of a lap, during practice' »

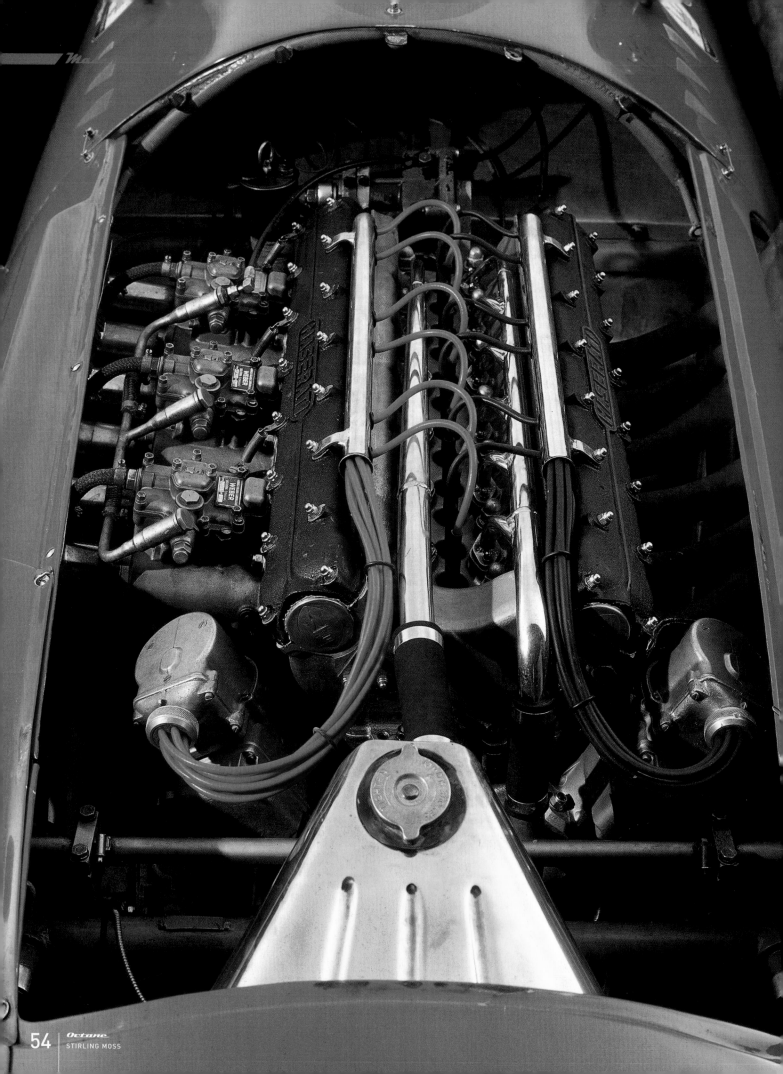

'As the flag fell, Stirling made a typically quick start, and 200 yards into the race was already a length ahead of Castelotti, with Schell and Fangio trailing some distance behind'

colleague Juan Manuel Fangio. Then he took advantage of the mid-lap garage to change to the fuel-injected five-speeder, but could not get near the time of his previous lap.

Practice ran from 4pm to 6pm, but most drivers had enough by 5.30pm. However, at 5.45pm Fangio took advantage of the almost empty track to turn in a lap time of 1min 44.2sec, putting him in line for the £100 prize. This spurred several other drivers into action as they tried to beat Fangio's time.

Peter Collins went out in Fangio's car but couldn't better the Argentinean's time, and then Harry Schell lapped his Vanwall in 1min 45.2sec, even though the British model was overgeared for Monaco. Realising the £100 prize was still up for grabs, Stirling rushed back to the Maserati pit, but found that the cars there were out of action; his faster carburetted machine was back at the garage halfway round the circuit.

Borrowing the Maserati of privateer Horace Gould, Stirling hurtled back to the works garage to collect his own car, rushed back to the pit for a plug change and set out to try and beat Fangio, but was 0.6sec slower – so Fangio got the prize.

The next day's practice time ran from 5.45am to breakfast, but none of the works Maseratis showed up and Peter Collins set fastest time of the day in his Lancia-Ferrari, while Saturday's practice, which started at the same unreasonable hour, saw Stirling again try both types of Maserati; again, the carburettor car was quicker. Imprudently, Maserati later lent their fuel-injection car to Louis Chiron of the Scuderia Centro-Sud, who had run the bearings of his own 250F by over-revving the previous day, and the heavy-footed Monegasque repaid the loan by passing the pits after a few warm-up laps

1956 Maserati 250F
SPECIFICATIONS

Engine
2493cc, in-line six-cylinder, twin overhead camshafts, two valves per cylinder, 12:1 compression ratio. Three Weber carbs

Power
270bhp @ 8000rpm

Transmission
Four- or overdrive five-speed manual, rear-mounted in unit with differential

Suspension
Front: independent via coil and wishbone, telescopic dampers. Rear: de Dion axle with transverse leaf spring and telescopic dampers

Brakes
Drums all round with finned aluminium cladding

Top speed
155-180mph, dependent on final drive ratio

with the rev counter almost off the clock, at which point the works engine disintegrated. The Maserati mechanics shrugged their shoulders and shovelled the debris into a packing crate; Chiron was out of the race.

So, too, were the BRMs of Brooks and Hawthorn, which had suffered valve trouble and were already on their way back to England. That left 14 on the grid: five Maseratis, four Lancia-Ferraris, three Gordinis and two Vanwalls.

With their engines revving, and the day hot and sunny, the drivers waited for the start of the grand prix. On the front row of the grid with Moss and Castelotti, Fangio stalled his engine, but fortunately it restarted easily. As the flag fell, Stirling made a typically quick start and 200 yards into the race was a length ahead of Castelotti, with Schell and Fangio trailing: a lead that he steadily extended.

'Brilliant and unflurried' was how *Autocar* described Moss's race: behind, there was chaos. Soon after the start, Trintingnant's Vanwall ran up the back of another car and bent its nose badly enough to restrict airflow through the radiator; it eventually overheated and retired. On the second lap, Fangio's Ferrari spun backwards onto the pavement on the Ste Dévote right-hander, where the course climbed back into the town, and started running downhill against the flow of the race. Schell's Vanwall clouted the side of the errant Ferrari, was bounced into the straw bales and spun into the wall, bending its front suspension, while Musso swerved into the bales and broke the steering of his Ferrari. Fangio regained control and set off in the right direction, leaving two angry drivers and two bent cars in his wake.

»

By the fifth lap, Moss had extended his lead, with Collins second in his Ferrari, followed by Behra, Castelotti, Fangio, Perdisa, Manzon, Gould, Bayol, Pilette and Rosier; an order that prevailed for several laps, during which Fangio got closer to Castelotti, who was reluctant to let him by. However, on the 12th lap Fangio nipped by on the chicane, which had been made sharper that year to slow the cars before they ran along the edge of the harbour, where the previous year Ascari had dropped his Lancia in the drink. Five laps later, Fangio reeled in Behra on the chicane, too; meantime, Castelotti had retired.

Then it was Collins' turn. He didn't ease up, but kept an eye on his mirror and left enough room for team leader Fangio to overtake if he could. Which he did on the 25th lap, but not before he had clouted the nose of his car. Driving furiously, he then hit the wall on the bend before the pits and damaged a wheel, but continued with Collins close behind.

After 40 laps, Fangio pulled into the pits to rest, handing his Ferrari to Castelotti, who'd walked back from his immobile car; 14 laps later Collins, who was maintaining second place behind Moss, was called into the pits and made to hand over his car to Fangio, who rejoined the race in third place behind Behra. These rather unjust team tactics meant Fangio drove three-quarters of the works Ferrari team in the race. By lap 60 he'd overtaken Behra and was lying 50 seconds behind Moss.

In lapping Perdisa, who was being slowed by a grabbing front brake, Moss buckled the nose of his car against his erratic team mate's tail: 'Hit Perdisa up the arse due to his braking on the straight,' he noted tersely in his diary.

Three laps later Perdisa made a brief pit stop and pulled out just in time to baulk Moss again on the Gasworks corner, forcing Stirling to take avoiding action. The earlier shunt had provoked one of Moss's bonnet catches into coming undone, but he kept going, as at that late stage of the race a pit stop would have let Fangio into the lead.

But while the frantic Fangio steadily gained on Moss's Maserati, Stirling maintained his lead, finally crossing the line at the end of the 100th lap to win the race by a margin of just six seconds from the hurrying Argentinean. Behra finished third and Castelotti, despite having made a pit stop to complain about 'the heap of wreckage' he had been given to drive (I bet it sounded better in Italian!), came fourth.

It was the first victory at Monaco by a British driver since the enigmatic Anglo-Frenchman 'Williams' back at the beginning in 1929, and that sustained lead from start to finish made this one of Stirling's greatest drives. More than 50 years on, how does he view renewing acquaintance with the Maserati that had given him such a clear victory?

'The cars we are driving today are not the same as when we drove them back then – they are better, which makes them easier to drive,' he says. 'And that's a pity!'

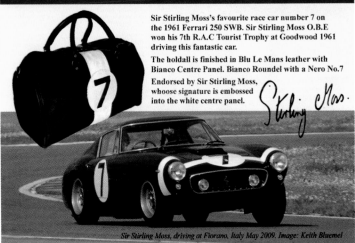

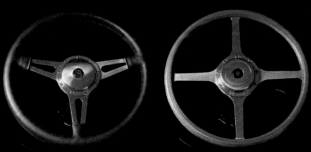

CLOTHES & FASHION

If it is true that clothes maketh the man then Sir Stirling's wardrobe is a lesson in understated confidence and restrained elegance...
Words and photography: Philip Porter

Sir Stirling has always dressed well. As with his driving, he is precise in what he wears and appreciates style. Indeed, he was once chosen as one of the 10 Best Dressed Men of the Year. In many ways he dresses conventionally, but he always gives it a Moss twist.

'I have my own taste,' confirms Stirling when asked if he has ever followed fashion. 'For example, I haven't had a jacket with pockets on the outside made for years. I just don't have mine like that. None of my clothes have pockets on the hip, because people stuff them and they look awful.'

Instead, he has inner pockets on both sides. If there is a danger of them bulging he carries his man-bag, talk of which leads him on to gadgets. The fertile brain is at work again...

Stirling believes there is the potential for a device whereby if you walk a certain distance away from your bag something, either in the bag or your pocket, makes a noise to alert you:

he has nearly left his bag on aircraft a few times. Also, of course, this device doubles as a security measure because it alerts the owner if the item is being stolen.

His jackets today are always single-breasted, but he wore double-breasted when he was younger. 'Of course, I generally wear a BRDC tie, too. That has always been an important club to me and I always wear their tie.'

He never wears a bow tie, other than with evening dress, because he cannot tie them! 'At the start of my career Mike Hawthorn wore a bow tie and so it wouldn't have been right for me to come along and do the same thing. So I have never really learnt to tie them. I do have a nice chequered flag bow tie for wearing with a tuxedo.

'I don't wear hats because my trademark is my bald patch really. It is more than a patch now – my bald top. I wear a hat at the Goodwood Revival meeting to be in period.'

Time is a consideration that is ever-present in the Moss

Clockwise from above right
No matter what the company, occasion or circumstance, Sir Stirling's wardrobe never lets him down. Understated his style certainly is, but it is also elegant and confident without being brash.
It is also interesting to note that Sir Stirling refutes the idea that he has ever been a follower of fashion, preferring instead to set his own agenda. The absence of embarrassing flares and flowery shirts only serves to support this idea.

Stirling's clothes

thinking. Buttons take time and are maddeningly slow to undo or do up. The Moss solution? Poppers. 'I wear a lot of shirts with poppers. On all my informal stuff I prefer poppers because I can just tear them off and that is it. Also, I usually have two breast pockets, but certainly I need one with my pen in it. That is an American thing where they give you space to put it alongside the main pocket.'

Any particular preference as to collars? 'Yes, reasonably wide. I don't use button-down because if you wear a tie you have to undo them, then do them up again. If you don't wear a tie, I can't see why you would need them. I do have shirts with a mandarin collar, where you don't need a tie, which I find quite useful.

'Underwear is quite important: decent, comfortable underwear and there are so many different types. I don't wear vests very often.

'I have all my trousers lined over the knee to stop them bulging. I always like two pockets either on the side or down the front, and at least one back pocket. I am wearing braces more now because I find that I fluctuate in size a bit and sometimes trousers are tight, sometimes they're a bit loose.'

Bearing in mind the importance of time to Stirling, he has only one pair of shoes with laces. As to socks: 'Always black. You shouldn't wear brown shoes after six o'clock, so every time I go out I would be chancing it, therefore I always wear black socks.'

He does not have particular favourite shops but has quite

Clockwise from top left
Sir Stirling has very particular views on the clothes he will and won't wear. Comfort and style are key to his philosophy. Quality and value for money are also high on the list of must-haves.

a lot of items made in Bangkok where he stops en route to Australia. He often buys shoes from Bally. I can personally attest to the quality and how comfortable they are, as he very kindly gave me a pair he could no longer wear!

Does Stirling frequent the clothes shops of London? 'No, too expensive really. I get some things, underwear and what-have-you, but other clothes I usually get in America. They have a tremendous selection over there.'

With his penchant for the fairer sex, did Stirling dress to impress or appeal to the ladies? 'No. I dressed mainly so that if somebody was with me they wouldn't feel embarrassed that I was over-dressed or under-dressed. In London, at the better clubs, you have to wear a jacket and tie anyway.'

Moss approves of this and describes himself as a traditionalist. 'Yes, very much. I find it difficult not to wear a tie when I go out. With my mandarin type of collar, that is OK; I can get away with that. Whether they would accept that at the RAC, I don't know. Jacket and no tie. I haven't put it to the test.'

When I say to him that he, of all people, might be accepted at the RAC without a tie, he responds: 'You see, I wouldn't want to do that.'

Clothes sum up a person's character and that sums up Stirling's. He knows precisely how he wants his clothes to be but he would never have the arrogance to assume he would be treated any differently from anyone else. He conforms but exudes confidence, though never over-stated.

Menswear for Racing Heroes

Suixtil
at life speed

AVAILABLE AT

ANDREW McDOWALL
GENTLEMEN'S TAILORS & OUTFITTERS
CHICHESTER, UK

ESCAPADE
SPORTS
CAUSEWAY BAY, HONG KONG

STRADALE
GALERIE AUTOMOBILE
VILLENEUVE D'ASCQ, FRANCE

WWW.SUIXTIL.COM

Mithril Racing

corporate driving days at Goodwood

Mithril Racing is the UK's most exclusive operator of classic car and super car driving days, conducted at the UK's most exclusive venue – Goodwood Motor Circuit.

In addition to letting your guests sample our mouthwatering range of sports and racing cars, you can even arrange for the maestro himself to host your day; Sir Stirling Moss, pictured left doing what he does so well – engaging each client personally before taking them for a high speed passenger ride.

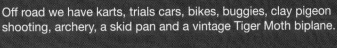

Off road we have karts, trials cars, bikes, buggies, clay pigeon shooting, archery, a skid pan and a vintage Tiger Moth biplane.

Quite simply our aim is to give your guests a day that is so enjoyable they will remember it, and you their host, for the rest of their lives.

mithril.co.uk

tel 01243 528815

Stirling's BRITISH *Winner*

Stirling's driving genius and Tony Vandervell's unshakable vision made for one of British motor racing's greatest success stories. Doug Nye explains...
Photography: The GP Library, Wouter Melissen/ultimatecarpage.com

ooking back on the momentous seasons of 1957-58, and his exploits in bearing magnate Tony Vandervell's now-legendary Vanwall Formula 1 cars, Stirling recalls: 'The Vanwall was terribly important for me. At last a British-built Grand Prix car capable of winning against anybody. But it did not do its winning easily... the engine had bad flat spots, the gearbox was bad and it was a car which demanded delicate handling, but very fast, with good brakes, and acceptably reliable.'

Damning with faint praise? Hardly – much of the Moss secret for success has always been his uncompromising frankness. In the definitive 'teardrop' Vanwalls, Tony Vandervell combined the best technology the world could offer. Just consider his contributors: chassis by Colin Chapman, aerodyne body shape by Frank Costin, 2½-litre 4-cylinder engine head and valve-gear derived from Norton racing motor-cycles, engine crankcase from Rolls-Royce, fuel injection by Bosch of Germany, disc brakes by Goodyear of America... Mr Vandervell's avowed ambition was, 'To beat those bloody red cars,' and the teardrop Vanwall was his means to that end.

At the May Silverstone non-Championship Formula 1 race of 1956, Stirling had given the latest Colin Chapman-chassised/Frank Costin-bodied 'teardrop' Vanwall its debut race. He promptly broke the Silverstone lap record, and scored the Acton marque's maiden race win. He, '...felt quite proud to be driving that car, but there was obviously still work to be done before the Vanwall became a real World Championship contender,' so he shone that year as Maserati's No 1 driver. By October, however, he would test the latest Vanwall and wrote in his diary just two words – 'Bloody quick'.

After signing to drive as Vanwall's No 1 in 1957 – with Tony Brooks his team-mate – he quickly submitted a long list of suggestions; improved dampers, larger rear brake discs, greater wheel movement, research into improving fuel economy. The 1957 'teardrop' Vanwalls emerged with tall coil-spring/damper Chapman struts at the rear, replacing the original transverse leafspring. Pirelli was withdrawing from racing tyre supply, Maserati and Vandervell prevailing upon them to continue old-stock supply through the new year.

At Monaco, Stirling crashed at the chicane while Tony Brooks finished second to score Vanwall's first points. By the finish, the ponderous Vanwall gearchange had left Tony's palm like raw meat. But Brooks then crashed his Aston Martin at Le Mans and Moss developed a raging sinus infection after attempting to water ski backwards off La Napoule on the French Riviera...

Roy Salvadori and newcomer Stuart Lewis-Evans drove the Vanwalls at Rouen and Reims. The latter – with his friend and advisor Bernie Ecclestone in tow – performed so brilliantly he secured a permanent No 3 drive with the team.

Stirl was discharged from the London Clinic only 48 hours before travelling to Aintree for the British GP. Tony was still battered and sore, and plainly would not last the race. Still

Above and left
Three Vanwalls line up on the Monza grid in 1957, all having qualified faster than 'Those bloody red cars'; the Vanwall team at its Aston works, circa 1957.

'At last a British-built Grand Prix car capable of winning against anybody… but it did not do its winning easily'

Above
Tony Brooks in the swansong Vanwall 'Lowline' at the 1960 French Grand Prix. This car, chassis 'VW11', was based on the winning 'VW5' frame of 1957-58.

they qualified on the front row, with Stuart barely a second slower. Stirl led away in his car 'VW1', and after 20 laps held first place by 9secs from Behra's Maserati. But then his engine began to misfire. The team had planned for Tony to hand over his car – 'VW4' – to Moss if necessary. In a 13sec stop they swopped. Tony soon retired the sick 'VW1' while Moss raced on in 'VW4'. On lap 69 he repassed Stuart for third. But simultaneously the clutch in Jean Behra's leading Maserati exploded and Mike Hawthorn's second-placed Ferrari punctured a tyre on the debris. Moss and Lewis-Evans in their green Vanwalls raced on, first and second in the British Grand Prix.

Within two more laps Stuart's throttle linkage fell apart, dropping him to seventh. But Moss and Tony Brooks emerged jointly as the first British drivers to win a Grande Epreuve in a British car since Segrave for Sunbeam in the 1923 French GP… 34 years before.

As a 12-year-old I was riveted to the TV coverage of that race – and the home win has resounded with me ever since. Sorry if such partisan emotion is unfashionable these days. Back then it was commonplace – and intensely real.

Tony Vandervell had achieved his first ambition: 'To beat those bloody red cars.'

But the Vanwalls were promptly humiliated in the German GP at the Nürburgring, where their taut suspension proved totally unsuitable. Stuart crashed, Stirl finished a distant fifth and Tony ninth. On the 17-mile road circuit at Pescara Stirling then drove 'VW5', passed Musso's Lancia-Ferrari '…and led relatively easily to the end. Apart from fluctuating oil pressure, which made me stop to add oil, the Vanwall never missed a beat.' Now Vandervell had beaten, 'those bloody red cars,' on their home soil.

At Monza for the Italian GP proper, Stuart Lewis-Evans then qualified on pole from Moss and Brooks. The Lancia-Ferraris were outclassed. The race became a straight fight between Vanwall and Maserati. But by lap 40 – despite early worries with a sticky gearbox – Stirling led Fangio's Maserati by 18 seconds, and 'VW5' boomed on to win Vanwall's third World Championship GP. Fangio was World Champion Driver, Stirling runner-up for the third successive year. 'If only I had not tried to water ski backwards at La Napoule… who knows what might have been the outcome…?'

Above
Hard-charging Moss with crunched Vanwall nose (he'd stubbed it on Phil Hill's Ferrari) at the 1958 Moroccan GP.

For 1958 a Formula 1 regulation change saw alcohol fuels banned in favour of maximum 130-octane aviation gasoline, or 'AvGas'. Pending full redevelopment of the engines to suit, Mr Vandervell ignored the late-organised Argentine GP opening the season... and Stirling won in Rob Walker's 1.9-litre rear-engined Cooper-Climax instead.

The Monaco GP marked Vanwall's reappearance, but none survived race distance. Eight days later, the Dutch GP at Zandvoort saw the Vanwalls 1-2-3 on the starting grid – the mercurial Lewis-Evans on pole again from Moss and Brooks. Stirling ran away from the BRMs to win in 'VW10'.

Tony Brooks in 'VW5' was then invincible in the Belgian GP at Spa, Stirling blowing apart his engine on the opening lap. Tony's touch through the high-speed swerves caressed his near neutral-handling, basically understeering Vanwall at shattering speed, beating Mike Hawthorn's latest Ferrari V6 into second place.

At Reims in the French GP, Stirl inherited second place behind Hawthorn's winning Ferrari after a frustrating and troubled race. At Silverstone he qualified on pole only to watch helpless as Peter Collins's Ferrari drew away into the distance, and then his Vanwall engine threw a rod... and burst.

Vanwall approached the German GP at the Nürburgring with meticulous care. While Hawthorn's Ferrari took pole position, Brooks and Moss joined him on the front row, with Collins's sister Ferrari outside them. Driving 'VW10', Stirling built an 18-second lead in three laps: 'I was using only 7000-7100rpm. I felt good and the car was simply splendid, handling beautifully. Then it seemed as if somebody had switched off the ignition. It was as sudden as that. The engine just cut, dead. A tiny screw inside the magneto had vibrated loose and fallen into the works, shorting it out.'

Tony Brooks responded magnificently, in 'VW4'. Fangio-like, from a long way back, he simply hunted down the leading Ferraris of Collins and Hawthorn. He closed with them, caught them and passed them both, to win. But Peter Collins crashed fatally in the effort to keep pace.

Moss in 'VW10' then dominated the Portuguese GP to win at Oporto, although the following Italian GP at Monza saw his gearbox break. There, despite an early stop to investigate an oil leak, Tony Brooks blazed through the field to win, in 'VW5', from Hawthorn and Ferrari's American new boy, Phil

Hill. The outcome of the World Championship competitions, for both Drivers and Constructors, was decided in the Moroccan GP at Casablanca. To earn the drivers' title Stirling had to win the race and set fastest lap – which in those days scored an extra point – with Mike Hawthorn finishing lower than second. In 'VW5' Stirl did everything asked of him, but with Hawthorn's Ferrari team-mate Phil Hill backing off towards the finish, Mike took that crucial second place – and became World Champion by one point. Vanwall, however, pipped Ferrari to the Constructors' Championship by 48 points to 40. 'Those bloody red cars' had been beaten well and truly.

But that deciding race of 1958 had also seen stark tragedy. Stuart Lewis-Evans's engine had seized at high speed and his Vanwall crashed into roadside rocks, bursting its fuel tank and exploding into flames. The slender young Londoner was so badly burned he died a few days later. Tony Vandervell had grown particularly close to Brooks and Lewis-Evans – not so much to Moss whom he regarded as the complete professional, a necessary talent but a most demanding one. In failing health with heart problems, the rugged Old Man decided his mission to put British industry on top of the Grand Prix pile had been accomplished, and accordingly – on January 12, 1959 – he announced his Vanwall team's withdrawal from serious Formula 1 competition.

Now this is really sad – indeed pathetic – but what this 13-year old did when he heard the news on the BBC Home Service was to take his team of Dinky Toy Vanwalls down to the bottom of our garden in Guildford, Surrey. I doused them in paraffin, and cremated them. Ten days later I would hear

Above and right
British Grand Prix, 1957 - Moss takes over Vanwall from Brooks; Moss at Melling Crossing.

that Mike Hawthorn had just been killed in a road accident, up on the Guildford bypass above us. I could scarcely absorb how much motor racing was changing… but it was engulfing me.

And at Goodwood for this year's Festival of Speed I could scarcely believe that I had been involved in 17 Festivals since a few of us dreamed it all up in 1992-93. And as the onetime teenage Vanwall fan I wanted to pinch myself as the boys pushed me off in 'VW5/VW11'. Sitting there you feel closely embraced by the cockpit sides and wrap-around perspex screen, though the space broadens 'down below'. My word, those warrior drivers' cochones demanded space! The tall left-hand gearchange is dog-legged left and back into first gear. The magneto switch is clicked to 'ON', the fuel cock is selecting 'ALL', and I have about a quarter-inch of throttle opening.

We're rolling well. 'G'on, Doug,' roars Scott George of the owning Collier Collection. I pop the clutch. BLAMMM! That magnificent 2½-litre fuel-injected engine fires, declutch, catch it all on the throttle, whoop, whoop and away to the Avenue start line.

Marshals wave me to the timing beam, and indicate the traffic light. Red. Jochen Mass has just blazed away in the 1937 Mercedes. I can smell its boot-polish fuel. Whoop! Green light, a sympathetic 4500rpm, clutch home – we charge towards the double-apex right-hander. Inwards-and-forward, second gear. Coo she's got some grunt! Feather throttle, Doug you really are not Moss, nor Tony Brooks. They won in 'VW5' in 1957-58, Pescara, Monza, Spa, Casablanca. This view, part-through, part-over the Perspex wrap-around was their's. This I can share. Their transcendent skill? Never.

Boot it past the House. Snatch back into third. BARK-clack-BARK!!! Bawl under the bridge, over the rise, brush the disc brakes at the brow, before you can see Molecomb Corner's deceptive 90-left. Heel-and-toe, clack forward, second again. Turn in, wood-rim wheel, feed in that throttle – and the teardrop-bodied design which became the first-ever British Formula 1 Constructors' Champion rockets into the hillclimb proper. Shave Goodwood's famous knapped-flint Wall, right at Carne's Seat, up another gear at the top left-hander, and under the finish arch in The Birdless Grove.

Just a taster – but what a car, for true-Brit enthusiasts of a certain age…our Vanwalls were the crown jewels – and the World Champions who had, indeed, beaten '…those bloody red cars'.

Top, above and right
Writer Doug Nye at the wheel of the Vanwall, Goodwood 2009, wearing borrowed helmets from Rick and Rob Hall after his own – predictably out of date – had been confiscated.

Stirling's road car...

ROAD CARS
I have owned

Stirling has had so many cars he can't remember them all – but then he has been driving for 74 years, starting on his father's smallholding before he semi-legally took to the road. Here he recalls just some...

My first car, which I didn't take on the road, was an Austin 7. I didn't drive it on the road because I was six years old! I took it round the farm but it was a road car of sorts.'

In 1936 Stirling's father, Alfred, had moved the family to a house called Long White Cloud, near Bray on the Thames. The house had some land and so Alfred modified the Austin 7, removing some of the bodywork to make it useful for carrying stuff around the small farm. This is the car in which Stirling learned to drive. He mapped out a small circuit which he used to hurtle around – all good experience. It even included a section of banking; his father had driven him around Brooklands when Stirling was aged five.

Morgan Three-wheeler
'Then I had a Morgan Three-wheeler, a 1936 Super Sports, with a Matchless engine.' It was intended as a 16th birthday present but Alfred actually bought it a little sooner. Stirling, though not 16, the minimum legal age for driving a three-wheeler, applied for his licence and it was issued, the

authorities having carelessly overlooked the fact that he was still 15. So, he was illegally driving legally!

The Morgan began to be used for transporting young ladies around. One day Stirling had the misfortune to roll the Morgan and was seen crawling underneath the machine looking for his passenger – on this occasion, his pet ferret.

MG TB
The three-wheeler was fun but rather confined. It was replaced by an MG TB which, although less sporty, was more suitable for enjoying the company of young ladies. For motoring excitement, Alfred allowed his son to compete in a handful of minor competitive events in the BMW 328 he had acquired from a fellow dentist. This only served to fuel Stirling's passion for motor sport, and a year later, in 1948, he acquired the little Cooper 500 that would start off his motor-racing career.

Morris Minor
'I think my next car was a Morris Minor, which I ran for quite a while.' When first acquired, it was a single dark and

sombre colour, but soon it was given a more racy two-tone colour scheme with the main parts of the bodywork now cream and the wings picked out in, very probably, Stirling's distinctive pale green, as used on his racing machine. There was a hand-operated extra spotlight positioned at the top of the driver's windscreen pillar – no doubt handy for bird-spotting at night. Moss's British Racing Drivers' Club badge was proudly mounted to the grille.

'On my Morris Minor, I remember getting a Derrington exhaust manifold along with a light alloy head, which made a certain difference. It helped the compression a bit, but probably not that much really. There was no sophistication in those days!'

Jaguar XK120 Fixed Head Coupé

After his breakthrough win in the classic Tourist Trophy in a borrowed XK120 in 1950, Stirling was invited to join the Jaguar works team being formed to contest events the following year. This led to a number of races in 120s as well as the pure racers, the C-types. In early '51 he acquired his own XK120.

'I had the 120 Fixed Head Coupé and it was a nice, good-

Clockwise from far left
The Minor in its original colour and sporting a spotlamp 'for bird-spotting'; Standard 10-engined 8 looks racy on Borrani wires; MG TB still with wartime paint edging; Morgan Super Sports.

looking car. I had a tow bar fitted because I was towing a caravan. I had a really nice caravan because I thought it would save me having to stay in hotels and also save some money.' One day the caravan, which was inclined to wander, started weaving violently on a downhill section, turned over and demolished itself – to say nothing of the six dozen eggs Stirling had stocked up with!

'The 120 Fixed Head Coupé was a good, long-legged car and suited me well. It had drum brakes originally, but I got a set of disc brakes from Dunlop Girling to put on my Maser 250F in '54, and had another set fitted to my road car.'

Stirling's two-tone Fixed Head was left-hand drive, as the factory was building this model only for export. This was particularly handy as he did most of his driving on the Continent, taking part in several rallies.

Mercedes-Benz 220A

'When I drove for Mercedes in '55 they gave me a 220A, which wasn't actually mine but I had it for the whole year and at the end of that year I bought it from the manufacturer at a very reasonable price.' The Mercedes cost £2123 to

purchase in the UK at that time, which compared with the Jaguar XK120 FHC at £1263. In addition, Stirling was paid a modest weekly allowance to have the car cleaned so it reflected well on the company. He cleaned it himself and pocketed the money!

Standard 8/10

'Then I also had a Standard 8 with a 10 engine and Borrani wire wheels. I had that for quite a long time. It was overkill, it really was!' Stirling liked the idea of what used to be called a 'Q' car, a car which looked mundane but was actually pretty hot. The engine had been tuned at Barwell Engineering and fitted with two large Solex carbs. The suspension was lowered, a Panhard rod fitted and competition linings employed. The interior was full of gadgets – something Stirling has always liked.

'It was small and handled quite well. It wasn't a very startling-looking car but it was really quite good, particularly as most of my mileage was around London; it suited me quite well for that. It was a wolf in sheep's clothing.' Stirling nicknamed this one 'the baby'.

Clockwise from top left
Stirling examines a Facellia – he'd had and enjoyed its big sister, the Vega. The 300SL 'Gullwing' with stripe for recognition, on the 1957 Tour de France; with the Mercedes 220A that he later bought from Mercedes. Famously, he drove straight home in it after the Mille Miglia.

Mercedes-Benz 300SL Gullwing

'Then later on I had a Mercedes Gullwing, a lightweight example with knock-off wheels. I think it was the first car, that I can remember, that had a go-faster stripe down the centre. I had the car painted and I had a white stripe down the centre, nearly a foot wide. I thought it was good for recognition purposes.

'The 300SL was a more exciting car to drive than the XK, but not as useful for the normal person. The Merc was a car that really and truly needed to be driven quite carefully, or quite well. With a Jaguar, it was a production car and handled that way. It was easy to drive.

'The 300SL kept you awake, that is for sure. It was quite a difficult car, particularly in the wet, with the swing axles. I must say it had good power, quite nice, heavy steering actually, and, of course, it had drum brakes not disc brakes in those days.'

Stirling competed in the Tour de France in 1956 and 1957, driving a 300SL on both occasions. It seemed the '56 car was borrowed from the factory but the '57 car was his own, prepared by the works. He was second the first year behind

de Portago in a rather more suitable works Ferrari and fourth the following year when he was up against no fewer than 11 Ferraris. The event, as it circulated France involving three road sections totalling 3400 miles, six circuits and four hillclimbs, was really tough on the cars.

'It was amazing we finished at all, with a persistent water leak, jamming starter, broken bumper and only top and second ratios left in the gearbox!'

Facel Vega

'A terrific car in its time for what it was. It had a large Chrysler V8 engine, air conditioning and a radio, and was automatic. It wasn't a sporty machine but it was very comfortable indeed. You would sit in luxury. It was very fast and great as a tourer. That is what it was: a grand tourer really, rather like the later Jensens.

'The Facel was a luxury car but very reliable because of the Chrysler engine and excellent gearbox. And it had electric windows! It was a super vehicle for what I used it for, and that was just to cruise from one race to another.

'In those days you could fly to Brussels £5 each way, so it

Above
Being collected, probably from Heathrow by Renault Caravelle in 1960. Moss says he used to leave his Facel Vega parked at Brussels Airport for a few days between races, when you could fly home for a fiver.

was £10 return. At Brussels Airport you didn't have to pay to park the car, so you could just leave it there. So I would do that and fly back home for a few days, then go back, pick up the Facel and drive on to the next race.

'It handled pretty well. It was a big car and very comfortable. You have got to remember that in those days that sort of model would do 140 at least and had disc brakes and everything, and petrol was so cheap it didn't really matter. It really was a very convenient car.'

Lotus Elite

'I was forced out of racing in 1962, due to my accident. I remember I then had a Lotus Elite, which was really a very nice car – except, of course, like all Lotuses, when you closed the door it was more likely to fall off than latch!

'It wasn't exactly a quiet or relaxing machine; it had a very good Climax engine! But it was such a nice-handling car; lovely. It had an automatic transmission, a really super gearbox. This was a prototype and I think it was the Hobbs Mechamatic.

'The car in general was pretty unreliable, yes. It was not a

very practical car to have but I wasn't driving around that much any more, like going to races, so it didn't matter.'

Opel GT

'I then had an Opel GT, which really was one of the most attractive non-events going. It was a good-looking car, with absolutely no real go or anything. A not particularly great machine in any way but it was quite reasonable looking.'

'Your secretary,' comments Susie Moss, 'used to cruise around in that Opel thing. Good looking.' Susie is presumably referring to the Opel.

BMW 2002TI

'I did have a BMW, a 2002ti, which was a very nice car.'

Stirling was famously patriotic and during his career would only race foreign cars if there was no viable British alternative. However, driving road cars made outside the UK did not seem to bother him.

'I didn't think it mattered in a road car. I thought that patriotism was for the country rather than for the cars that country built.'

Mini

'I had a Mini, with all sorts of different extras and gadgets on

Above
Jaguar had tow bar fitted for the purpose of towing a caravan. Unfortunately, one day said caravan decided to go on a wander and flipped, destroying itself and six dozen eggs Stirling had earmarked for future breakfasts.

it. I remember I had a thing that would automatically light a cigarette.' 'That was 1968,' adds Susie. 'You used to pick me up in that. It had no seat for me and I had to sit on the floor!'

It might seem odd that Stirling, who was one of the original jet-setters and enjoyed a glamorous lifestyle, mixing with the wealthy in the world's most desirable settings, was not always buying the latest exotic sports car or prestigious saloon.

However, he counters: 'You have got to remember that I was in the lucky position where every week during my career I was racing a car of some description. Half the time at least it was a sports or touring machine. Therefore, the idea of getting into a really nice road car like a Ferrari or a Porsche or a Jaguar was really wasted on me.'

When asked if he was a car enthusiast, as well as enthusiastic about racing, Stirling has this to say: 'No! I think that I knew what I wanted or needed from a car. I like to have a decent radio and for it not to be too noisy inside. Although some of the vehicles went against that, like the Lotus for example.

'I wasn't doing much mileage a year really. I did when I was racing, of course, but I was living in central London. I would go up and see my family, about 30 miles away, but I didn't often drive to places. I would usually fly or get picked up.'

MOSS
THE GLORY YEARS

The latest, and probably last, in the series of Stirling Moss Scrapbooks fills in the gap between the 1955 and 1961 editions of these acclaimed and very different motor racing books

I t all started with the *Stirling Moss Scrapbook 1955*, which was published some 50 years later in 2005. Majoring on his amazing season with Mercedes-Benz, when Moss became an established international star with his first Grand Prix win and fabulous victories in the Mille Miglia, the TT and the Targa Florio, the book allows readers a real insight into his amazing lifestyle and collection of original scrapbooks.

Moss was unique, for a sporting star in those days, in that he appeared on the front pages of the newspapers as well as the sporting pages due to his colourful lifestyle. The second in the series was the *Stirling Moss Scrapbook 1961*, which again featured a single, great season during which he clocked up brilliant victories against the Ferraris at Monaco and Nürburgring. This book was followed by the one covering his early years (1929-54), which is featured on pages 22-28. Here we now have a taste of the latest in the series which looks beyond the races and behind the scenes and, with over 50 pages from his diaries, positively reeks of period atmosphere.

Left
This was the big breakthrough for British Formula One constructors and started the country's long dominance that can be traced right through to Brawn and Red Bull today. At Silverstone in '56, Moss won with the brand new Vanwall and this gave him the confidence to sign with the team for 1957.

Picture Post, May 5, 1956

Stirling Moss uses a NENETTE

"WITH MY NENETTE I CAN DUST, CLEAN AND POLISH ALL IN ONE GO IN RECORD TIME"

Once over with the Nenette Dust-Absorbing Polisher, and the dirtiest car is spotlessly clean, with brilliant showroom-sheen. No hard work, no water, no separate polish; the fringes are impregnated with Nenetol. Take a tip from STIRLING MOSS, and get a Nenette to care for your car. **13/9**

An Autoclean Product
LEXINGTON PRODUCTS LTD., 2 LEXINGTON STREET, LONDON, W.I. (GERRARD 8600)

Right
Moss had a love hate relationship with the Lotus 18. The brilliant Chapman-designed machine alternated between bringing him some of his greatest triumphs and trying to kill him. He won the Watkins Glen GP in '60, the first of four races in the USA in October and November.

Above
It has often been said that Stirling was the first commercially-minded racing driver. In reality he was the only British driver to attempt to make a living purely from racing. The rest either had other professions during the week or were in the motor trade.

'The Lotus 18 alternated between bringing Stirling

Right
This is the Maserati 350S attempting to end the lives of Stirling and Denis Jenkinson. According to Stirling's diary there is a 300 foot drop below.

1956

Below
The press tried to make out there was hostility between rivals Moss and Hawthorn. Though very different people, nothing could be further from the truth. Here Stirling shows Mike his latest 'toy'.

Right
For the Reims 12-Hours which accompanied the French Grand Prix, Stirling shared this 'Bobtail' Cooper with a young American by the name of Phil Hill. It was a frustrating race for the pair; Moss led for the first eight laps and then constant misfiring necessitated numerous trips to the pits.

Left
Stirling loved films and was often to be seen at premieres. He went to the theatre less regularly, even though he lived close to the West End. Here he takes time to chat with actresses Patsy Lancaster and Hermione Harvey.

Below
Art and engineering combine in the Maserati 250F: Moss drove the iconic single-seater for the last time in the Argentine GP, in early '57, where he set the fastest lap. His diary later revealed he was ordered not to 'try and beat Fangio'.

1959 HONOURS FOR THE ARTS & SPORT
Alec Guinness—Knight
Stirling Moss—OBE

Right
Of all those honoured in 1959 by The Queen, the newspapers chose to highlight the brilliant actor Alec Guinness and the country's favourite sportsman, who was rarely out of the limelight.

some of his greatest triumphs and trying to kill him'

»

Above
The moment that changed Grand Prix racing for ever: Stirling acknowledges the flag as he takes the first, mould-breaking win for a rear-engined F1 car in a Grande Epreuve.

Right
Stirling and first wife, Katie, were testing a Mini-Minor when they had a head-on accident which put them in hospital. The judge made an example of Moss and banned him.

STIRLING MOSS SHOULD NOT HAVE BEEN BANNED

THE suspension of Stirling Moss's licence for 12 months is a wicked thing. It will cost him thousands of pounds. He is not an accident-prone driver. There are dangerous drivers who get away with a fine.

Stirling Moss is a skilful and prudent driver. As I read the evidence he made a wrong decision and it is a hundred to one he will not do so again. J. A. Marshall, Saltdean.

*school.
When I was five I thought your name was Steering Moss becos you steered so well. But I am six now.
We all hope you get better soon and become the World Champion
Lots of Love
FROM
Yasmine Ghandhi*

Above
In '59, Stirling purchased a Cooper-Monaco which he debuted at the British GP meeting. When an oil pipe broke and the cockpit filled with smoke, one paper ran the headline: *Stirling Moss escapes from blazing car at Aintree.*

Left
This little girl said she cried when she heard Stirling had been hurt (at Spa in 1960 when a wheel came off his Lotus).

Left
As happened in those days, Moss drove a whole raft of different cars during a season, including a Formula Two Borward-engined Cooper in the distinctive Rob Walker colours.

Right
Heat exhaustion caused Moss to retire from heat one of the Buenos Aires City GP, but after a few reviving gulps of milk he managed to complete heat two.

Milk revived Moss after heat collapse

Right
Difficult to know exactly what Stirling is up to in this Italian newspaper cutting, but it is clearly a new gadget and no great hardship examining the young lady's left leg.

'Fangio was kidnapped by rebels but persuaded them

MAY 1957

Sunday 12

3rd after Easter   (132-233)

Godfrey's birthday

Up at 4.30, food + to start.
Took off at 5.37 + 35 mins +
12 kms later, the accelerator broke.
All ok after a trying few
seconds! To Brescia, food etc etc
etc, + watched results coming in.
Food & bed at
11.30 pm.

Poor Fon + Edmund were killed
to-day, 20 odd mls from home.
Also 12 pers.

Right
In 1957 and 1958 the Vanwall took Moss to some great results. Here at the Nürburgring, in 1957, the bumpy and undulating nature of the uniquely-challenging circuit did not suit the car and even Stirling could only finish fifth.

Above
Page from Stirling's diary recounts the tragic day that spelt the end of the Mille Miglia. The Marquis de Portago, known as 'Fon', was killed together with his friend Ed Nelson, plus a number of spectators. Moss's own race lasted less than five minutes.

Left
Sebring,1958: Stirling took the lead in the works DBR1, then suffered a flat tyre. Co-driver Tony Brooks took over and built a slight lead before he had to pit to change the brake pads. Stirling then reduced the deficit to the leaders, of over a lap, to just 14 seconds before the gearbox cried, 'enough'.

Right
Moss at work around the streets of Monte Carlo in an F1 Cooper, 1959. He is rounding what was originally the Station Hairpin, became Loew's and is now simply, and unimaginatively, the Grand Hotel Hairpin.

Left
Many of Stirling's conquests were air stewardesses. Here he indulges in the art of the chat-up from the cockpit of a pristine DB3S Aston, examples of which he would race during 1956.

to leave Moss alone as he had Katie with him'

Left
Here Stirling pilots an Aston Martin DBR. Presumably, due to the lack of numbers, he was testing. But where and when? Answers on a postcard, please, to philip@porterpress.co.uk

Above
When Stirling had his massive accident at Spa, in 1960, the get well messages came from far and wide. This one is from Giles, the famous *Daily Express* cartoonist and car enthusiast.

Right
Having achieved maiden victories for the Vanwall and Cooper marques, Moss made it a hat-trick when, in 1960, he did the same job for Lotus. He is seen here at Monaco rounding the famous Gasworks Hairpin with the harbour in the background.

Left
Stirling really enjoyed the Coopers because they could be hurled around and, unlike their great rivals, bits rarely fell off. Ironically, on this occasion, at Silverstone in 1960, the suspension broke.

Above
Note the number seven. Not only is this Stirling's lucky number but it also indicates he was one of the very first to be issued with a competition licence after the war.

Right
In the build up to the Cuban GP in Havana, Fangio was kidnapped by Castro's rebels and held until after the race to publicise their cause and fight against the Batista regime. Fangio persuaded them to leave Moss alone as he had Katie with him.

Fangio kidnapped on eve of big race: police guard on Stirling Moss

Above
In late 1960 Stirling went out with actress Judy Carne who was making a name for herself in the West End before heading for the States and becoming famous as the 'Sock It To Me' girl in *Rowan and Martin's Laugh-In*.

Above
Stirling, in Tommy Sopwith's Equipe Endeavour Mark 2 3.8 Jaguar, chases Roy Salvadori in John Coombs's example. Roy won by a whisker.

Right
When there was a chance Moss would lose his road licence he took out a US licence to enable him to continue to race, which proved to be a good move.

Moss: I am American for race purposes

Pictures, cuttings and information in this feature are all taken from Stirling Moss Scrapbook 1956-60. It is published by Porter Press International at £34.95, ISBN 978 1 907085 00 0.

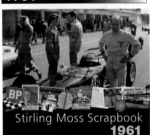

Aston Martin
DBR1

No other Aston Martin has achieved the motor sport success of the DBR1. No other Aston provokes the same appreciation from now legendary drivers. Here's how it feels when pushed hard, and why it feels that way Words: Mark Hales Photography: Ian Dawson

'The revs rise and you need a big dose of opposite lock, and for that you need a well-braced torso and strong arms'

ASTON MARTIN'S DBR1 and Jaguar's D-type were fellow countrymen locked in a titanic battle for Le Mans which would surely bring sales in the showrooms. And, at a glance, they even look similar. Long bonnet, oval air intake for the radiator and humps to clear the tall 16-inch wheels, vestigial doors that flex and bend as you pull them shut, then leave your shoulders feeling exposed. Like products of the time.

But look again, only more carefully this time. See that the Aston has a slightly more delicate appearance. The curves are longer and more gentle and the whole car looks smaller, seems to sit lower overall, which makes it look wider and more ready to hug the ground. The result is a body described as 'one of the most beautiful of all sports racing cars', made from wafer-thin 20-gauge aluminium, rather than the D-type's 16-gauge, as part of a quest for lightness and woe betide anyone who moves to lean or sit, or the photographer who makes ready to attach a camera sucker. Then as you look closer still, you begin to notice the engineering differences under that swooping skin, the design inspiration that could be the key to success on the track but which had to be built and tested to be proven.

You see that the DBR1 has a spaceframe chassis made of welded steel tubes rather than the D-type's aircraft-style monocoque tub. The tubes criss-cross the cockpit floor and have to be spanned by a sheet of plywood to support the heels and, whereas you sat low down in the D-type, nicely trapped between transmission tunnel and sill, in the Aston you perch in a vestigial seat – borrowed in this particular case from a DBR4 Grand Prix car – and only because that was better than the yet flimsier original which still graces the passenger side. Then the transmission tunnel seems impossibly slim and surely not large enough to contain something like the Jaguar's tough four-speed gearbox, an impression confirmed when you can't find a gearlever sticking through a hole. Instead the lever sits level with your left knee, short and stubby like a single seater's, and when you lift off the boot lid you discover this is because it leads via a rod to a five-speed gearbox and differential which is mounted at the back, driving the rear wheels via a pair of double-jointed half shafts. It was then that I began to realise just how different the Aston was from its fellow Brit.

Whereas the D-type could claim all sorts of advanced engineering features, like a riveted monocoque, dry sump lubrication, all-synchromesh gearbox and aluminium disc wheels, the overall layout was simple and conventional. Big, tall iron block engine in the front, four-speed gearbox in the middle and a big beam axle at the back hung on five simple links with traditional double wishbones for the front suspension. Simple, proven technology, all of it built with the extra needed to guarantee stamina.

»

The DBR1, though, has that magnesium-cased transaxle between the rear wheels, just like you'd find in the tail of a Maserati 250F or Birdcage or a BRM V16 Grand Prix car and, like those three, the Aston boasts five dog-engaged gears instead of the Jaguar's four. The aim is to equalise weight distribution in a front-engined car although the downside is that the propshaft always spins at engine speed.

There's de Dion rear suspension too – something that Jaguar apparently tried but rejected in favour of that big beam – with telescopic shock absorbers and a Watts linkage for lateral location, and links to operate the torsion bars, which run forward along the cockpit floor, the ends just visible to the sides of the seats.

Back in the cockpit, you see that the right-hand sill covers the exhausts, which jut out just below your elbow while the left is filled with the battery and two separate oil tanks, one to feed the gearbox and another for the dry sump engine, which holds no less than 20 litres. Obviously the designer didn't want oil starvation to be an issue in a long race but they wanted to reduce the effect of weight on the handling by putting it in the middle.

Now lift off the bonnet and, as you do, notice the rows of neat catches which remain flush until you poke a finger at them, whereupon they obediently rotate inwards and click open. Feltham, where the Aston was made, was close to the centres of English aircraft production and many of the Aston workforce came from there so that's what they knew. Although it's detailing which takes more work than two bolts and a leather strap, the catches secure a panel against a passing airflow but open quickly and provide no opportunity to lose a clip. Exactly as they would on the aeroplane from which they were borrowed.

The engine that all this reveals was specially made for the car rather than derived from a production model like the Jaguar's and it is lighter thanks to an aluminium block instead of iron, but it is smaller in displacement (3 litres rather than 3.4). It looks physically smaller too, sits lower and the magnesium cam covers don't shine like the bare aluminium ones from Coventry so it doesn't quite dominate the underbonnet ambience in the same way. Two plugs per cylinder rather than one are fired by separate distributors driven from the back end of each camshaft and although you could argue that this would keep you going if you lost a plug or a rotor arm, it probably had more to do with flame travel in a hemispherical combustion chamber and the need to get the mixture burnt effectively.

The advantages of the Aston's front suspension layout are rather harder to determine, though, because where you might expect to find the accepted geometric ideal of double wishbones, instead there are large trailing links, the top ones

operating a lever arm shock absorber rather than the much better telescopic type used at the back, which were adjustable even by 1959. Then you see that each bottom link operates a transverse torsion bar running across the car. Just like a Beetle...

Trailing links are an esoteric choice for front suspension which was favoured by the pre-war German manufacturers, so possibly this was a legacy carried over from Auto Union designer Professor Eberan-Eberhorst's original DB3 of 1951. It's all beautifully made, cast and forged, with roller bearings everywhere and neat offset bushes and splines for all the various adjustments, but it is undeniably complicated and it's hard to see why they did it like that other than because they could. Or maybe the Jaguar was only simpler because it was made on a line and built in volume for any comers with a cheque good enough for £3878. Seventy D-types sounds a lot compared with just five DBR1s, all but one of which were exclusively factory cars.

Our subject is DBR1, chassis no. 2, winner of five world championship events between 1957 and '58. Since 1993 it's been owned by the same arch enthusiast who drives it on track days but for the serious competition employs former Formula 3000 driver turned historic racer Peter Hardman. Preparation is by Tim Samways' Bicester-based Sports and Historic Car Engineers and, inevitably, since the car is regularly used in competition, Tim and his team have been responsible for some development, which he says has been more in pursuit of reliability than outright performance. The last decade's continuous race programme would have made unreasonable demands on heads and blocks made nearly 40 years before and the exclusivity of the engine meant that replicas had to be cast and machined. Thanks to some logical extra fettling and some new camshafts, the result is about 285bhp – or 25 more than they ran in the shorter races, 40 more than the lower-stressed Le Mans-spec and about the same improvement as modern-day tuners have wrought from the Jaguars.

The Aston's engine, though, revs considerably higher. In the day the drivers used 7000rpm, close to Ferrari V12 territory and about 1500 more than allowed by Jaguar, and when you consider that the Aston weighs about 1900lb against the Jaguar's 2400 (and assuming that all the weights and measures are honest) the Aston's oft-quoted power disadvantage against the D-type doesn't sound so much – although Ferrari may have been a different matter. Samways has also improved »

'Thanks to some logical fettling and new camshafts, the result is about 285bhp - or 25 more than they ran in the shorter races and 40 more than the Le Mans-spec'

the gearbox with some different dog rings because although ideal in theory, he says the 'box was not thought very pleasant to handle at the time. The Maserati item which it resembles is a delight, with a shift so light and fast the lever might not be connected to anything. Samways says the Aston factory did fit one to the DBR1 as an experiment but then reverted back to the DB version when what they should have done is dismantled the Maserati 'box and found out what made it better.

The suspension is also a fair bit stiffer than it was with bigger torsion bars and a fair amount of work to the internals of the dampers. When Hardman first drove the car, he felt it was too soft and that didn't allow him to slide the car about and point it how he wanted, so the changes were made and the car is several seconds a lap quicker than it was. Some of that will be the tyres which although to original 16-inch width and pattern will have the benefit of more modern rubber compounds, and some will be the engine but I've never been able to understand why they didn't try stiffer set-ups at the time – or if they did, why it didn't work. But, enough of the technical stuff, and time to see where the car's advantage might be...

The replacement seat still has a back that is too vertical for me to be comfortable but it does boast another improvement in the shape of extra brackets to stop it flexing, because just as I have also discovered so many times, Hardman found he couldn't brace his body properly and ended up hanging on to the wheel just when he shouldn't be. And yet again, I just don't know how they managed at the time, especially as they wouldn't have had the full harness on which Hardman, quite sensibly, also insisted. Flick the switches salvaged from an aviation parts bin and press the starter. Hear the musical wail overlaid with a searing crackle that only six cylinders arranged in line can make. Wait an age for the temperature in the vast quantity of oil to lift the needle on the gauge, then reach down for the stumpy lever, which falls straight into the palm. Lift the spring-loaded catch that guards first gear slot (the gate is modern-conventional with first left and forward and the catch is another Samways improvement which stops an enthusiastic shifter finding first instead of third...) and off you go.

Which turns out to be easy. The clutch (which is on the back of the engine) is smooth, and the gears – once the oil circulating from the tank has also warmed a little – are also easy. The gate is maybe not quite so well defined as the Maserati's but the lever's movement is minimal, maybe six inches in total, and the faster you throw it, the less effort it takes and the smoother the shift. It is definitely a fingertip rather than a clenched fist activity and so much faster than the Jaguar's change, which makes you wait for the synchros to catch up. The engine, meanwhile, is smooth and revvy and needs to be kept between five and six-eight for it to work best whereas the Jaguar's pulled from about four, but then it needs to because it has a four-speed

Right
Interior is set up for racing, not beauty. The driver's seat is not original but borrowed from an Aston DBR4 Grand Prix car.

'Feltham was close to the centres of aircraft production, and many more of the Aston workforce came from there'

'Now lift off the bonnet and, as you do, notice the rows of neat catches which remain flush until you poke a finger at them'

Above left
Rear bodywork lifts off to reveal the transaxle, a defining characteristic of the DBR1's design.

'box. One would be the recipe for an ultimate quick lap when you were sharp, but the other would get you out of trouble when you were tired... Decisions, decisions.

But what of the handling about which the drivers of the day were united in their approval? You can hear the creaking and groaning from the suspension as you ease out of the pit area, even above the rasp of the engine and the whistling whine of the transaxle that rises behind you, and the car now feels very stiff indeed, following each ridge and rut with faithful accuracy but as you up the speed it begins to flow. You can tell a lot about cars – particularly historic ones – from the first response to the wheel; does it roll as a whole or does it sit or sag at one end or the other? Is there lost motion when you straighten up, the kind that will add a bit to any input you make? And the brakes, the essential that compromised so many of these cars? The DBR1 has Girling discs all round with dual circuits which were standard at the time and, with the benefit of modern fluids and friction materials, are firm and powerful.

The Aston turns out to be an unusual mixture of ancient and modern, and not just because of the brakes and more modern spring rates but because the response to the wheel is instant and the car rolls as a whole – like the C-type I raced last year, only sharper. But then almost immediately the Aston takes a set without your asking, yaws its tail about five or ten degrees to the side. It's another familiar characteristic but, once again, the DBR1 seems to do it more quickly and there's no wait for the inertia to build. Then you have to hold that yaw with a dose of power, tickling it more and more through the corner

until you are flat by the exit. Too little and the car will lose its yaw and start to push at the front. Too much and it begins to slither wide.

When it does, you hear the inside rear tyre give up the struggle and start to spin. The revs rise and you need a big dose of opposite lock, and for that you need a well braced torso and strong arms. Hardman had Samways speed up the steering so he could catch the car, but it ups the effort and I'd be interested to know how heavy it was for Brooks and Moss. As it is, if you have to summon that effort, your momentum is gone anyway and it's a fine line you have to tread.

But the difference between this and, say, the D-type, is the speed of response. The D makes you wait, slides further but makes it easy to sort out. Lets you play like the feline it is, but doesn't have the claws if you overstep the mark. And the difference between others – like the GTO – which need to be drifted to keep up the momentum, is the balance. You have to lift the GTO and put it where you want it, manage the mass to get it going. The Aston does that for you and it does seem that the lower overall weight, the light engine and gearbox in the back for 50/50 weight distribution, are a major factor.

In a sprint race there would be no question, but driving it like that for 24 hours... You would of course, because that would be your job and you wouldn't think about it any more than they did. Or would you rather sit low in the calmer cockpit of the D-type and use the engine's low down punch to close the gaps between four gears? Tricky. I could let you know at about 3am.

THE
Comeback
KID

A master at turning adversity into triumph, some of Stirling Moss' most glorious moments came in races where it must have seemed all was lost

Words and photography: Philip Porter

Winning from flag to flag is impressive: it shows complete domination and superiority. Perhaps even more amazing, though, is the scenario that involves some handicap early on which delays the competitor and means the odds are now heavily stacked against ultimate success. The drive through the field, involving much overtaking and pushing to the limit, is the stuff of legend. It creates drama and excitement, is the ultimate challenge and a mark of a true champion, a man who never gives up, fights to the last and forces himself and his machine to beat the odds and steal that almost impossible victory.

Stirling Moss sealed his fate in destiny and the pantheon of the greatest sporting stars by defying the odds again and again, and showing he was a true 'racer' – a man who is never beaten.

That didn't mean victory was always the outcome, due probably to some mechanical fault, but he had undoubtedly conquered the field when he left it.

1958 Nürburgring 1000Kms
Aston Martin DBR1 with Jack Brabham

After retiring in the Monaco GP and winning the Dutch GP the two preceding weekends, Stirling was at the uniquely-challenging Nürburgring with the Aston Martin team for the 1000 kilometres (625-mile) sports car race in late-May, 1958.

Three DBR1 Astons were ranged against four V12 Ferraris and three Jaguar D-types, plus sundry Porsches and a field of some 50 cars in total. The lesser classes even included a Peugeot and Volvo, 'a menace to themselves as well as others,' stated Moss at the time.

Mike Hawthorn's Ferrari was faster than Moss' leading Aston in practice but Stirling made his usual lightning Le Mans start and had a 100-yard lead when the cars doubled back past the pits. Apart from the Ferraris being faster, Stirling's additional handicap that day was Jack Brabham. Though only a year away from winning his first World Championship, Brabham was still learning the ropes and was new to the DBR1. He was well off the pace.

Stirling had a 12-second lead after the first lap, which increased to 14 after the second. Hawthorn's Ferrari was second, followed by Tony Brooks in another Aston, 'Taffy' von Trips (Ferrari) and Roy Salvadori (Aston). By the end of the third, the Moss lead was 21 seconds.

Breaking the lap record on each of his first ten laps, Stirling handed over to Brabham with a 60-second lead. 'We managed the change-over very quickly, in six and a quarter seconds, with the car still rolling and both of us more or less in it at the same time.'

Jack Brabham, being unfamiliar with the car, lost the lead within a lap and after three was back in third. He was soon brought in and Stirling sent off to hunt down the big Ferraris. He didn't take long to catch von Trips and then overhauled Hawthorn. By lap 22, the halfway stage, Stirling led by over two minutes. From lap 25 Brabham did another five circuits and, when he pitted, the leading Hawthorn/Collins Ferrari, which had closed right up, stopped at the same time.

Moss once again showed his supremacy. By pushing himself and the car hard, he had built a lead of over four minutes by lap 33. The flag fell on the Aston after seven hours 23 minutes 33 seconds of motoring at an average of 84.26mph. The Ferraris took the next four places.

'It was a fine victory for Aston Martin and I had enjoyed every minute of it. When it was over, I was quite ill and felt completely beaten up; I had done too much driving - 36 laps [over 500 miles] of the 44. It took me just on a week to get over it, even longer than it took me to get over the Mille Miglia. My pulse rate when I got to bed that evening at the Sporthotel was 130, but I learned a lesson from it: I would not do quite so much another time.'

Clockwise from above
Moss looking relaxed and fully the master of the DBR1; team mates Moss and Brabham enjoy the laurels with David Brown, the Aston Martin 'patron'.

1959 Dutch Grand Prix
Cooper-Climax at Zandvoort

The Dutch Grand Prix which took place in 1959 was one of the races in which Moss suffered from the Colotti gearbox which blighted his season. Stirling was driving Rob Walker's 2½-litre Cooper, now fitted with double wishbone rear suspension for the first time. In practice, with a head-on wind down the straight, he was getting 6750rpm in fifth gear, a speed of 150mph plus.

In this race, the handicap was provided by Moss himself. Though sitting on pole, he most uncharacteristically made a dreadful start.

'It was Bonnier's BRM which led first time round from Gregory's Cooper, with Brooks' Ferrari third chased by Schell, Brabham, Behra and Graham Hill, all ahead of me. Gregory passed Bonnier to take the lead and for several laps they fought it out with Brabham watching it all in third place. I was sixth on lap 12, and Graham Hill in the Lotus and I were being baulked by Behra, who was holding us up badly.

'Not until lap 24 did I scrape past him into fourth place, and then ran right away from him to try to make up the third of a lap I had lost on the leaders whilst trying to pass the Ferrari. On lap 34 I was 11 seconds behind Bonnier. By lap 40 I had reduced this to eight seconds. On the 49th lap, I passed Jack into second place and closed up on the BRM. On the 60th lap I was through into the lead, with just 15 laps to go.'

Once again, it had been a great comeback drive but this one was not to have a happy ending. With just 12 laps to go, he was out with a broken ball race in the bell-housing. Though there was no glory on this occasion, it had still been a terrific drive and proved, if proof be needed, Stirling's pre-eminence once again.

Clockwise from right Getting ready for the off; Moss' Cooper-Climax menaces Jean Behra's Ferrari.

1959 Nürburgring 1000Kms
Aston Martin DBR1 with Jack Fairman

In 1958, Moss had to regain the lead and later build one when his advantage had been wiped out by his slower team mate. A year later, he chose Jack Fairman to partner him as Jack was fast, reliable and consistent rather than outstandingly quick. This one was really to stretch Stirling.

To add to the pressure, he had done a deal with Aston Martin, which was intent on concentrating on Le Mans a fortnight later and the resultant publicity value should they be successful. Aston would enter a single car at the 'Ring if Moss covered the expenses should it not win. Knowing Stirling's 'careful' attitude to financial matters, this was, as he now admits, pretty rash!

So, there was just a lone Aston against the might of Ferrari and Porsche. The DBR1 was far from new and, in fact, 1959 was the third successive year it had done this event, triumphing in the previous two. The Ferraris proved quicker in practice. However, Moss made his usual brilliant start and led by 15 seconds after the first gruelling lap.

For his first 16 flying laps he was under his 1958 record and built up an incredible six-minute lead. However, when Jack Fairman took over, it began to rain and made the conditions even more challenging. Luckily, Fairman was a highly experienced driver but he was not in the very top league. Then, disaster. One of the cursed slower competitors got in his way and forced Jack off into a ditch. It looked impossible. The rear of the car was beached.

Now, as a young lad, Jack had worked for his father's laundry business. This often involved carrying very large and heavy baskets of clean laundry up several stairs to the upper floors of commercial premises. As a result, Fairman developed exceptionally strong back muscles. Thus he literally lifted the rear end of the big Aston Martin out of the ditch. Meanwhile, back in the pits, Stirling had given up hope and had started packing away his skid lid, goggles and shoes when someone yelled that Jack was on his way in.

Clockwise from above
Despite its age, Moss was still able to extract Ferrari-beating performance from the DBR1; some in-car light refreshment.

Stirling yanked poor old Fairman out of the driving seat and set off with a 77-second deficit.

'I thoroughly enjoyed it from that moment on. Here, I thought, was a good excuse for me to have a go; if the thing broke people would not say, "He's a car-breaker." They'd say, "Oh boy, he had a go." I went after the two Ferraris and started dicing. I took the lead again on lap 29 and built it up again to plus two minutes by lap 33, when I gave it back to Jack for two laps. Once again the Ferraris went at him and, when he came in on lap 35 for me to do the final nine laps, Phil Hill was 22 seconds in front.'

Once again, Stirling pushed hard. Once again, the Aston responded and held together. By sheer brilliance, he caught and passed the flying Ferrari to take a fabulous victory for the duo and Aston Martin. Plus, of course, he didn't have to pay the expenses.

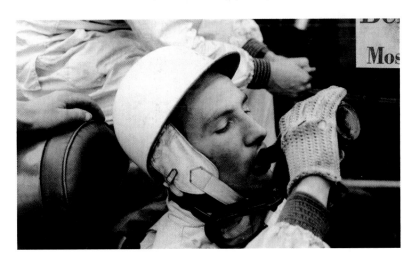

Above
Moss and Maserati during what he regarded as one of the greatest drives of his life at Buenos Aires in 1957.

Right
Moss' third victory in the Nürburgring 1000Kms, for the Camoradi team, was against all the odds.

1960 Nürburgring 1000Kms
Maserati Tipo 61 (Birdcage) with Dan Gurney

For the 1960 Nürburgring endurance race, Stirling was paired with American Dan Gurney to drive a Birdcage Maserati, entered by 'Lucky' Casner's Camoradi team. Stirling and Dan had already suffered from their lack of professionalism at Sebring. When Stirling drove the car in practice on the Friday at the 'Ring, 'the brakes and the handling were awful and it was overgeared by at least 500rpm.' Gurney only did two laps on the Saturday before an oil pipe broke. It did not bode well.

As this was a World Sports Car Championship event, the field was a strong one with Porsche and Ferrari well represented. Piero Taruffi was in charge of the pit organisation for the Camoradi team and so it was to be hoped that the chaos of Sebring would not prevail again.

Moss led from the start in miserable weather. It was misty and there was a fine drizzle falling. Team mate Masten Gregory was running second in the other Camoradi car but was soon relegated to third by Bonnier in a Porsche. By lap 15, when Stirling handed over to Gurney, they had a lead of two and a half minutes over Phil Hill in the Ferrari,

the Porsche having dropped to third. Gurney maintained the lead but then came major problems. He was forced to pit on the 18th lap with a broken oil line. The lead had become a half-lap deficit before Dan was able to rejoin. He then drove superbly in the rain and fog.

By the 24th lap, he was one and half minutes behind. This he had reduced to 47 seconds by lap 25 and three laps later they were back in the lead. However, he then had to pit and hand over to Moss. This dropped them to third.

Stirling then put in another of his storming drives to work back up to second and then, with just eight of the 44 laps to go, regained top spot, a position he held until the flag. The master had done it again, building a three-minute lead on the Bonnier/Gendebien Porsche, with Allison, Hill and Mairesse third for Ferrari. However, Moss magnanimously gives fulsome credit to his co-driver who well and truly pulled his weight as well. For Stirling, it marked a hat-trick of wins in this most challenging of events.

1957 Buenos Aires 1000Kms
Maserati 300S

At the time, Stirling considered this his greatest drive. The Buenos Aires 1000 kilometres was a sports car race in which he was to partner Fangio with the new 4.5-litre V8 Maserati 450S. The organisers had decided to run the race on the difficult Costanera circuit. It was 6.3 miles in length and the straight doubled back on itself so, in effect, there was a two-way traffic system with cars going both ways at around 160mph. As if this was not dangerous enough, the circuit was also unmarked and very bumpy. After Fangio had lapped at around 114mph, an artificial chicane was introduced to reduce speeds.

'When the flag fell, the 450S simply streaked away from the Ferraris, and by the 10th lap I was a good 60 seconds ahead of Masten Gregory. By 30 laps I was two and a quarter minutes up. The car called for a considerable amount of discretion in its handling on this circuit, which was a difficult one, with high-speed corners as well as slow ones. Because of its tremendous acceleration and maximum speed, I could have gone much quicker if it had been necessary. I was called in at the 33rd lap and Fangio took over the car and, by the 48th circuit, he had lapped the entire field except for Castellotti, who had taken over from Gregory about the same time as I handed over to Fangio.'

However, this supremacy was not to last. On the 57th lap, the transmission decided it'd had enough. The clutch-operating mechanism had broken and Fangio had been changing gear without it, which was too much for the gearbox. Castellotti went into the lead, with the Behra/Menditéguy 3-litre Maserati lying fourth.

On the 65th lap, this Maser was called in and Stirling took it over. He started to give chase to the Ferraris, who counter-attacked by calling in Castellotti on the 67th lap and giving his car to Musso whilst Castellotti took over the de Portago/Collins car.

'Oddly enough the 3-litre was a car far more suited to the circuit and much easier to handle, although not nearly as quick. Anyway, I found it a lot easier to drive the 3-litre on the limit than the 4.5, and actually made the fastest lap of the race with the slower car, which could really be thrown around. By 88 laps I had gone through to second place and was on the same lap as the leader, Musso. But, despite his failing brakes, I just could not catch him, and when the flag fell at the end of six hours on the 98th lap I was 80 seconds behind him. It had been a wonderful race and one I enjoyed immensely, culminating in a tremendous ovation from the crowd, who had, it seemed, enjoyed my drive almost as much as I had.'

Once again, glorious victory had not quite been the final result but nevertheless it was one of Stirling's finest moments.

1955 Tourist Trophy at Dundrod
Mercedes-Benz 300SLR with John Fitch

In this epic, Stirling had several handicaps to overcome. Once again, his co-driver, the very amiable John Fitch, though competent and experienced, was not seriously quick. And the opposition was tough too, with Mike Hawthorn in a works Jaguar D-type and Juan Fangio in another 300SLR.

Stirling took the lead during the first lap, while Hawthorn and Fangio enjoined in another of their famous battles behind the flying Moss. Stirling had built up a comfortable cushion when a sudden drama changed the whole picture. He had the exciting experience of a tyre suddenly throwing a tread while he was doing over 100mph. The flailing tread ripped into the right rear wing. Stirling nursed the car back to the pits where the mechanics cut away the damaged wing, changed the wheel and John Fitch took over.

Fitch was steady rather than rapid and was losing ground to local man Desmond Titterington who had taken over from Hawthorn. After six laps, Fitch was called in by an anxious Alfred Neubauer, the celebrated team manager, to be replaced by Stirling. He was now more than three minutes behind the leaders and had some serious work to do. Luckily it began to rain which helped Stirling, who soon caught Fangio's co-driver, Kling and then pursued the leading Jaguar.

Meanwhile, there was some consternation among the other teams, in particular Jaguar, as to how the Moss 300 SLR, with an exposed rear wheel which rendered it more like a Formula car, was allowed to continue. In fact, although the International Sporting Code required cars to finish intact, the TT regulations didn't included this stipulation.

At 50 laps, Titterington pitted to refuel and hand over to Hawthorn. This allowed Moss to close to within 25 seconds. With a full load of fuel

and Hawthorn taking a while to get back up to speed, Stirling was able to catch and take the D-type, but then he had to pit himself. This allowed Hawthorn to regain the lead but when he came out again. Stirling was just nine seconds behind. Within a lap, he had taken Mike again who shadowed the Mercedes initially but Stirling was soon able to build a lead he managed to keep until the end. Poor Mike Hawthorn, who had driven a valiant race, suffered a broken crank on the penultimate lap.

Autosport described Stirling's performance as 'one of the most brilliant drives ever seen on a road circuit.' He had overcome the conditions, a slow co-driver and a burst tyre, to say nothing of the psychological setbacks.

Above
Despite major damage and protestations from other teams as to the legality of racing with this level of damage Moss went on to win at Dundrod.

Left to right
The Vanwall crosses the finishing line first, to the delight of the Aintree crowd; Moss enjoys the jubilation.

1957 British GP at Aintree
Vanwall with Tony Brooks

Moss had joined the Vanwall team for a full season in 1957, with the British Grand Prix the third Grande Epreuve of the season. The first, the Argentine GP, had not been contested by Tony Vandervell's team and the Monaco GP had lasted just three laps for Stirling, as his brakes had failed, although team mate, Tony Brooks, managed to finish second. The team went to Aintree for their home GP without a win. Indeed no British car with a British driver had ever won the British GP.

The two Vanwalls of Moss and Brooks occupied the front row of the grid with Behra and Fangio in Maseratis. Stuart Lewis-Evans had been drafted into the Vanwall team to face the four Ferraris and seven Masers. He was on the second row.

Behra led initially but Moss was ahead when they crossed the line the first time. By the 25th lap, he had a lead of nine seconds. Then his engine went off song and he pitted. He rejoined but was soon back in. The rules allowed drivers to swap cars in those days and he had an arrangement with Brooks, who was far from fully fit having had a nasty accident at Le Mans a few weeks previously.

Accordingly, Brooks came in and handed over his car to Stirling. 'I tried to bundle him out of the bloody car, poor bugger, and then get back in and into the race.'

Moss was now ninth. By the 30th lap, he was up to seventh. He gained another place when he took Fangio four laps later. Another six laps and he overtook Musso for fifth. By lap 46, he was ahead of Collins and now in fourth place. That left him under a minute behind Behra, who was leading, followed by Hawthorn and Lewis-Evans. Behra set a new lap record but a couple of circuits later, Stirling had beaten it.

He passed his team mate for third on lap 69. At the same time, Hawthorn suffered a puncture running over some debris left by Behra when his clutch fell apart. Both were suddenly out. Stirling was so often the victim of bad luck but for once it was on his side and he was thus leading the British Grand Prix with 20 laps to run. On this occasion nothing went wrong and he and Brooks became the joint victors.

'It was a very proud moment because it was a British car and all that sort of thing, with a big, big audience there, of course, at Aintree.'

The victory at Aintree meant that Moss and Brooks were the first British drivers to win a Grande Epreuve in a British car since 1923.

1955 Targa Florio
Mercedes-Benz 300SLR with Peter Collins

Having taken the first three places in the Tourist Trophy, the Mercedes-Benz team had a mathematical chance of wresting the 1955 World Sports Car Championship from Ferrari at the last event of the season, the unique Targa Florio. They needed to finish first and second; nothing less would do. The redoubtable Herr Neubauer persuaded his directors to enter the team and the mighty Mercedes machine headed for Sicily.

With so much at stake for Mercedes, they needed a strong line-up of drivers. Rather curiously, Neubauer asked Stirling to decide with whom he would like to share a 300SLR, and also for him and Ken Gregory to suggest another driver. Stirling had no hesitation about choosing Peter Collins, provided he could be released by Aston Martin to whom he was contracted but who were not entering this event. Collins, though something of a playboy off the track, was a deadly serious competitor once behind the wheel. He had shone in the little 500s and sports cars but had not yet made his mark elsewhere so it was quite a bold suggestion. As to the other driver, Stirling and Ken came up with a driver who had impressed them at Dundrod where he had been sharing a D-type with Mike Hawthorn. Desmond Titterington, a native of Belfast, had shown great skill and determination, and was to prove another sound choice. Together with Fangio from the Argentine, genial American John Fitch and German Karl Kling, it was certainly a very international line-up.

Once the decision had been made, the whole force of the Mercedes over-organisation swung into operation. They invaded Sicily three weeks in advance with eight cars for practice, eight trucks, 45 mechanics and a positive fleet of touring cars. In contrast, Ferrari turned up with three cars and eight mechanics.

To enable the Targa Florio to qualify for the World Sports Car Championship, the distance had been extended from the usual eight laps to 13 circuits; over 500 gruelling miles (800 kilometres) and some 10,000 bends. The first driver was not allowed to do more than five consecutive laps and the second driver had to do a minimum of three laps. Ferrari planned to make four pit stops to change drivers, due to

the extreme psychical challenge of the course. Neubauer decided his drivers had to manage with two stops. Fangio thought four laps was the most any driver could manage but Neubauer was adamant they must try and do more.

The smaller cars started first with competitors being flagged away at 30-second intervals. On his first lap Stirling set a new lap record of 44 minutes and passed 16 cars. Castellotti in the leading Ferrari clocked 45 minutes 15 seconds. Stirling's next lap took 43 minutes seven seconds, the first ever 100 km/h lap. However, halfway round the circuit, mud from the recent rainstorms was making the circuit very difficult. Stirling was now two minutes ahead of Castellotti and three minutes ahead of Fangio.

Then, disaster. Stirling lost control on the mud, smote a bank and went over the edge. Thankfully, it was not quite the precipice he feared it was. However, he landed in a field, strewn with boulders, nine feet (three metres) below the road. The car was relatively unscathed but he could not get any grip. Photographers and others miraculously appeared from nowhere to help and, after several attempts, he managed to regain the track and rejoin the race, after retrieving his crash helmet, which blew off as he accelerated away. Most of the water had boiled away, he had lost eight minutes and was lying fourth.

He made it back to the pits where Collins took over the battered machine. Peter then proved his worth. He completed his first flying lap in 43 minutes 28 seconds. After five laps, the 350SLR was back up to third, with Castellotti leading Fangio. Collins then smote a wall but, somehow, got away with it.

After seven laps, Fangio's co-driver Kling led Castellotti's co-driver Manzon by eight seconds with Collins now just 36 seconds in arrears. Stirling took over again and even including the pit stop did an amazing 43 minute 41 second lap to regain the lead, just over a minute ahead of Fangio. Moss then upped the pace, going quicker and quicker to win an amazing race by more than four minutes. Fangio finished second as a result of Castellotti making an extra pit stop.

This time the handicap was driver error but, aided by the brilliant Peter Collins, Stirling more than made up for the rare mistake. It had all paid off and Mercedes-Benz triumphed in the Championship.

Above
The battered and bruised 300SLR after Moss' unscheduled flight in it.

1959 Tourist Trophy
Aston Martin DBR1 with Roy Salvadori, Carroll Shelby and Jack Fairman

As had also been the case in 1955, the World Sports Car Championship all depended on the final round. This was to be the classic Tourist Trophy race held at Goodwood and was of six hours duration, pitting the British marque against full works teams from rivals Ferrari and Porsche. Ferrari led the championship with 18 points, Aston Martin had 16 and the Porsche team were just a point behind. Moss was paired with Roy Salvadori, probably the quickest of the Aston team drivers after Stirling. They made a strong duo and Stirling took the lead, followed by team mate Shelby. All looked good. The cars even had hydraulic jacks fitted to speed up the wheel changing, the Astons being heavy on their tyres.

Then it all went dramatically wrong. Salvadori, who had taken over the leading car, came into the pits to refuel, fit a fresh set of rubber and hand over to Stirling. Some fuel slopped over the hot exhaust and the car became a mass of flames. Salvo leaped clear, landing head first on the grass and snuffed out the flames by rolling on the ground. Meanwhile, the refuelling tank in the pits went up and set fire to a pile of tyres. Luckily the circuit fire engine soon had it all under control.

Within four minutes of all this drama, Fairman, in the second DBR1, was called in and it was handed to Stirling, who had a job to do if Aston were to take the Championship. After three hours, he lay second to Bonnier in the Porsche, with the Trintignant Aston third and then the first of the Ferraris. Another half hour saw the Ferrari up to third place and, more importantly, Stirling had caught and passed the Porsche. Then he had to pit again and with two hours to go the Porsche led. However, hurling the big Aston round the Sussex circuit, the maestro caught the Bonnier/von Trips Porsche, overhauling it and gradually establishing an unassailable lead.

The battle may have been over but the war was not. The third-placed Ferrari, with Brooks at the wheel, was rapidly catching von Trips in the fleet little Porsche. The Championship hinged on their final order but 'Taffy' managed to hang on by a handful of seconds and Aston Martin, thanks to another inspiring drive by Stirling, won the campaign.

Clockwise from above
The burnt-out DBR1 in the pits; Moss en route to victory for Aston Martin.

Postscript

Stirling has been likened to a gallant knight in shining armour, sallying forth into foreign lands and conquering all against the odds. He certainly relished a challenge and was never better than when the task seemed an impossible one. But then he was no mere mortal.

It is interesting that he performed these feats more often in sports cars than single-seaters. Maybe the sports cars were built more strongly which allowed them to be pushed to the absolute limit for longer; certainly Stirling says they could be thrown around more.

It is fascinating, but hardly surprising, that many of his great drives took place at the most difficult courses for they allowed his skills full rein. Dundrod was narrow, twisty and considered highly dangerous. The Targa was just amazing with its lap distance of over 40 miles, making it a challenge to learn. The Nordschleife circuit at the Nürburgring was awesomely complicated as anyone who has driven round will attest. It must have been the ultimate challenge with its 172 corners per 14-mile lap. Stirling was quite simply the king of the 'Ring.

It is telling that this feature could also have been titled *Mission Impossible*, *Against the Odds*, *Achieving the Impossible* or *The Real Racer*. Any and all would have been appropriate.

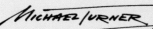

MOSS

Art

It's small wonder that the man who made such an art form of racing should himself have been immortalised by other artists...
Words: Richard Gunn

Left
Sebring Heat by Klaus Wagger; the 1957 12 Hours with Fangio in the Maserati 450S and Moss in the 300S. Stirling won his class and came second overall.

Above
New Kid On The Block, Alan Fearnley's atmospheric recreation of Roy Salvadori, David Brown, Stirling Moss, John Wyer and Reg Parnell viewing the new DBR1 at Aston Martin's workshop in Feltham in 1956.

Right
A stark and striking image, by Charles Mayer, of Moss and navigator Jenkinson in Mercedes-Benz 300SLR number 722 on the 1955 Mille Miglia, en route to setting a course record with an average speed of almost 100mph.

Below
Another Lap Record, by Bill Neale, captures Moss in action behind the wheel of an Aston Martin DBR1.

Right
Bill Motta's visualisation
of Moss in the 'Eldorado
Maserati' sponsored by
an Italian company for
the Monza Challenge.

Above
Wearing the Green by Michael
Turner shows the HWMs
of Stirling Moss and Lance
Macklin leading the works
Ferraris on the opening lap of
the 1951 Grand Prix of Genoa.

Left
A magical shape that will be forever associated with Moss; that of the Mercedes-Benz 300SL in this sculpture by Richard Pietruska.

Above and right
Two different takes on Moss
at the 1955 RAC Tourist
Trophy, Dundrod, Northern
Ireland; Alan Fearnley's
painting of Stirling's 300SLR
dicing with Mike Hawthorn's
Jaguar D-type at the hairpin,
and Debra Wenlock's view of
the same location showing
Stirling Moss' silver Mercedes
lapping the Austin-Healey
100S of Ernest McKillen.

Above
Stirling Moss slides his DBR1
out of the chicane at Goodwood
to win the 1959 Tourist Trophy
and clinch the World Sportscar
Championship for Aston Martin
in this Graham Turner painting
entitled *Goodwood Glory*.

Left
Tim Layzell's stylish 'Pop Art'
portrayal of Stirling Moss
driving the Rob Walker-
entered Ferrari 250GT SWB
to victory at Goodwood in
the 1960 Tourist Trophy race.
He is seen blasting through
the chicane in pursuit of
Roy Salvadori's Aston Martin
DB4GT which took second
place at the event.

»

Above
Klaus Wagger's acrylic on canvas capture of Moss and Jenkinson in Mercedes-Benz 300SLR number 722 on the 1955 Mille Miglia. This work was originally conceived as a poster proposal for the 2004 Mille Miglia event.

Right
Another Tim Layzell creation, *Moss the Magnificent*, showing Stirling climbing into the cockpit of an Aston Martin DBR1 as he takes over from Jack Brabham at the Nürburgring in 1958. He is watched by team manager Reg Parnell and Aston Martin general manager John Wyer.

Stirling's FERRARI

Legendary British racing driver and iconic Italian car: this star pairing dominated GT events in the early 1960s – and now they have been reunited

Words: David Vivian Photography: David Vivian, Gus Gregory
Archive photographs: LAT, David Castelhano

APRIL 30, 2009: Ferrari's Fiorano test track, Italy. Despite the near-perfect disguise, this is not just another day in paradise. Easy mistake. Under a warm sun, the echoing doppler wail of a 6-litre V12 blows through the complex on a gentle breeze, and our three-lap slot on track in the car generating it – the chassis-optimised 599GTB Fiorano HGTE – is due in about half-an-hour's time. I've had worse Thursday afternoons.

But whatever I imagine the immediate future holds – and fanciful notions of impossibly late braking and balletic drifting are a dogged delusion – it's all about to become a trivial sideshow. 'Iconic', 'legend' and 'history' are words that require considerate handling at the best of times, especially in such evocative surroundings, so I'll write the following sentences with extra care.

At 3:27pm precisely, the heavy iron gates at Fiorano's entrance slowly part and two more cars are waved through. The first is an iconic Ferrari with an exhaust note so resonant and loud that, even trundling towards the pit lane, it drowns out that of the fully exercised 599 on the track. The second is a chauffeur-driven Maserati Quattroporte with a British motor-racing legend riding in the rear. The icon and the legend go back a long way. When they team up again on Fiorano's hallowed tarmac in a few minutes' time, history will be made.

It was 58 years ago, in 1951, that Stirling Moss and Enzo Ferrari first shared the same newspaper column inches. Astute talent scout that he was, the Commendatore sent Britain's best racing driver a telegram offering him a go in a 2.5-litre Ferrari for the Bari Grand Prix in September. But when Moss arrived on the Adriatic coast for

Previous pages
Stirling Moss is reunited in Modena this year with Ferrari 250GT SWB no. 2735 GT – and takes the chequered flag for the 1961 RAC TT at Goodwood in the same car.

Below
Forty-eight years after he raced the car, Moss drives 2735 GT once again – now back in its original 1961 Rob Walker team colours – at Ferrari's own test track.

'Enzo wanted nothing more than to get Moss behind the wheel of one of his cars'

Clockwise from top left
Moss' first drive in 2735 GT was at Le Mans, 1961 – note NART logo; passing the grandstands at Brands Hatch en route to winning the 1961 GT race (below); on the grid for the '61 Nassau TT, his last race in 2735 GT.

his fitting, what he supposed to be his car, wasn't. Ferrari had changed his mind and decided to give the drive to Piero Taruffi. This flashpoint, it has been suggested, set Stirling's jaw for much of the rest of his racing career. Not only did he blank Enzo Ferrari on a personal level, he also vowed to do everything in his power to 'beat those red cars'. He was as good as his word and, for the next decade, he proved a major thorn in Ferrari's side.

Yet the schism wouldn't last: 'The thing was, I was really annoyed with Ferrari,' Moss will later tell me. 'He screwed me up by giving the car he said I'd be driving to Taruffi. I didn't think that was on and it took me quite a few years, with my cap in hand, to go and see him.' In truth, Enzo wanted nothing more than to get Moss behind the wheel of one of his cars, and he lined up a drive in a 156 F1 for the 1962 season, factory supported but run by, and in the dark-blue and banded-white colours, of Rob Walker.

The horrific crash driving a Lotus at Goodwood in March '62 that almost cost Moss his life and ended his career at the top tier of motor sport intervened. But before that door closed came a short but epochal period when the names of Moss and Ferrari would be closely linked with one more word: success. It began in earnest at Goodwood in 1960, where Moss, driving for the Rob Walker team, took a 250GT Short Wheelbase Berlinetta (SWB) to victory in the Tourist Trophy. Further reparations to the relationship with Ferrari ensued the following year when, in September, Moss went down to the factory to work through the details of his proposed F1 drive. While he was there he took up the offer to test a new Ferrari GT car at Monza, a development

Ferrari 250

Above and below
2735 GT has been totally restored by Ferrari Classiche to 1961 condition; it made a cameo on 1962 Goodwood programme but had been sold by Rob Walker in late '61.

mule which would go on to become arguably the most famous and beautiful road-going Ferrari of all, the 250GTO.

But it was in the hardly less exquisite SWB that he would dominate GT racing for the rest of '61, and he'd later describe it as the greatest GT car in the world. In truth, he was referring to one example bearing the chassis no. 2735 GT. As with the 250 he drove the previous year (chassis no. 2119 GT), it was supplied new from the factory in the distinctively Scottish colours of its entrant Rob Walker. In the model's first outing at Le Mans in '61, entered by Luigi Chinetti's NART team and with Moss partnered by Graham Hill, it retired after ten hours when an errant fan blade sliced through a water hose, causing the engine to overheat.

Despite the disappointment of a DNF, Moss relished the race for two reasons. First, in a nose-to-tail battle with the Aston DBR1s of Roy Salvadori and Jim Clark, he came to appreciate how special the SWB really was. And second, he worked his way up to third overall when it started to rain, leaving the works Testa Rossa of Parkes and Mairesse in his spray.

The records may have shown a faltering start to 2735 GT's racing career, but the way Moss drove the SWB gave every indication of what was to follow: a golden run of five successive victories, including a seventh Tourist Trophy for Moss at Goodwood and culminating with the Nassau Tourist Trophy in the Bahamas, the last Ferrari win of his career before the crash at Goodwood the following year.

Although car and driver had forged one of the great partnerships in motor sport, it was time for them to go their separate ways, Moss to pursue his business interests, 2735 GT to race on – in the gifted hands of Innes Ireland, among others, and for a while looking rather different. After a racing accident in 1962, it acquired a pseudo GTO body by Drogo which lasted until the early '80s when, after another scrape and generally looking much the worse for wear, this was removed by a UK specialist and replaced with new bodywork to the original Scaglietti GT Berlinetta short-wheelbase design.

But it was the man who bought the car a couple of years later, Clive Beecham, who is pivotal to our story. Clive was of the opinion, quite rightly, that although he now owned 2735 GT he was merely the custodian of a genuine slice of motor-racing history that should be preserved for posterity. He introduced 'the

'It was in the hardly less exquisite SWB that Moss would dominate GT racing for the rest of 1961'

GOODWOOD
INTERNATIONAL MOTOR RACING
MONDAY 23rd APRIL 1962   First Race: 1.30
OFFICIAL PROGRAMME 2/6

DRIVER OF THE YEAR – STIRLING MOSS!

old warhorse' – which had been raced, crashed, repaired, patched up and twice rebodied over the years – to a gentler but still active existence. And, in late 2007, he decided to go the whole hog and have it restored by Ferrari's in-house restoration facility, Ferrari Classiche, to its authentic, pristine glory in every detail, using the factory's original chassis blueprints and the services of Ferrari's engine foundry to cast a new block to replace the non-original unit fitted in 1967.

At the same time, the original Weber 46s were refitted, the transmission and differential overhauled, and all worn or non-original components repaired or replaced with original parts. Where authentic spares were no longer available – such as pistons and connecting rods, camshafts, gear-selector forks, aluminium-riveted fuel tank and exhaust system – replacements were made from scratch using drawings pulled from Ferrari's extensive archives.

And right now, on this glorious day at Fiorano, Sir Stirling Moss is climbing out of the Quattroporte to be reunited with the Ferrari in which he won most races, exactly as it was when he first 'took delivery' at Le Mans in 1961. Moreover, the reunion is taking place in the only way that matters a damn to a born racer: on the track. The early laps are tentative. Moss has never driven round Fiorano before. In fact, this is the first time he has been back to Ferrari in over 20 years. His last visit was to present his young son to Enzo shortly before the Old Man's death, the early antagonisms long buried.

But as Moss familiarises himself with the circuit, so the speed builds, the flashes of brake light get shorter and the angles of body lean greater. Soon, the animal bark of the 3-litre V12 is washing over the whole Fiorano complex. Stirling and the SWB are flying. At the end of his session, he reports that the car is almost exactly as he remembers, save for the pedals seeming slightly wider spaced (making it more difficult to heel 'n' toe). He doesn't need to say much more. Now, as 48 years ago, he lets his driving do the talking.

Below
Moss drove 2735 GT in the 1961 Nassau TT – he had a home in Nassau – and won by 83 sec from the second-placed Bob Grossman, in an identical Ferrari.

Next day, over an espresso or three in Modena's old town, I ask Sir Stirling what it was like driving the SWB and he is more forthcoming. 'It's a fantastic car. Really very nice to drive. The great thing about it is that it was always a pretty easy car to drive. Cart springs on the back, so very pedestrian suspension really, but very good nonetheless.' Understated to the last. △

Sir Stirling Moss on...

The Ferrari 599GTB Fiorano HGTE
'It is amazing the amount of adhesion they can now get from a production car. If you haven't experienced it, it's quite remarkable. You can behave like a complete hooligan and still get away with it!'

Racing
'I still love racing. I don't know when I am going to stop. I think I will stop when I feel I'm getting in other people's way, which would be a bit embarrassing. But at the moment, I don't think I am.'

The car he races now
'I've got an OSCA FS372 which, I must say, is absolutely stunning and just exactly what I want. It's 1500cc. I had a C-type which I sold. That's a fairly serious car. My competence level now fits 1500cc sports with drum brakes, and I really do enjoy the car for what it is. It's very fast and very stable, and I really enjoy driving it.'

Commuting
'For getting around, I've got a 50cc scooter with a Japanese tuning kit on it. It's got a windscreen that goes right over the top. If I've got to do a long distance I go by train anyway. There's not much pleasure in going on the road.'

The pill Fangio gave him before the Mille Miglia
'I still have no idea what it was. I can only think it was something like Dexetrine. A race for 10 hours is a long time. Mentally, it's a long time.'

What made him so good?
'I think it was that I could get to my fastest speed very quickly. If I knew a circuit, I could go out and in two laps be going as fast as I could. And I could keep it up – I was very fit.'

This year's stand-out F1 driver
'The lead Jenson's got now [at time of writing] is going to be difficult to take away. He's bloody good; the car's bloody good. I think it will get more difficult for him as the season goes on. What Ross Brawn has done is amazing. Of course he had the time to do it, but his worth was proved already, actually.

'Vettel is very good, too. I think you can tell how good a driver is only by looking at number two. This is why I find it difficult to find a place for Michael Schumacher. Schumacher was really terrific when he was with Benetton. When he got to Ferrari and had the best car, we never had a fast driver against him.'

F1 and the FIA
'The FIA has always buggered about with things. Once it said: "Right, because of safety, we're going to limit engines to 1500cc unsupercharged." Ridiculous! Really, that limit was a disadvantage. It's much easier to drive a lesser-powered car than a really powerful one. It didn't work. And it wasn't any safer, either.'

Top ten
BEST RACING CARS

Sir Stirling has piloted a broader range of cars than probably any other racing driver – and here he reflects on which provided the best memories
Words & pictures: Philip Porter

1 Mercedes-Benz 300SLR

'The 300SLR was very rugged and durable. It felt the most unbreakable car I ever drove in competition and was, I guess, the most reliable: I never had to retire a 300SLR. Of the six events we did with the sports car in 1955, four were absolute classics and I managed to win three. And we would have won at Le Mans if the Mercedes directors had not decided, wrongly in my opinion, to withdraw the cars some hours after the dreadful accident that claimed the lives of over 80 spectators.

'In the two lesser events, the Eifelrennen at the Nürburgring and the Swedish Sports Car Grand Prix at Rabelov, I finished a close second behind my team leader, Juan Fangio. In Germany I suspected the dampers had broken because the car started sliding a lot, but I still took fastest lap and we finished a metre apart. In Sweden, I took the lead but waved Fangio past. In those days we had team orders and there was no fuss about it. Fangio was number one and I knew my place. We finished with joint fastest lap and, in spite of something hitting me in the face and smashing my goggles, which necessitated a hospital visit after the race, I finished three-tenths of a second behind him.

'Of the three major events I won, none was a piece of cake. The Mille Miglia was probably my most famous win and I was very proud to conquer the Italians on their home soil. We were only the second non-Italian duo to win and this was the 22nd running of the 1000-mile race.

'As is well known, Jenks [Denis Jenkinson] and I had devised a system of what today are called pace notes which we had on one long roll of paper in a small box with two rollers and a window. This enabled »

Right
Le Mans 1955 was a sure-fire win for 300SLR, until terrible accident saw Mercedes pull out of race – a decision with which Moss strongly disagreed. Team mate Fangio took the first stint.

us to compete on a more level playing field against the locals, who knew most of the roads. The Ferraris were quicker on acceleration, as I found when following Castellotti early on, but he was driving solo, saving weight, and had a 4½-litre engine, as opposed to our 3-litre. I could catch him on the straights where we were reaching a genuine 170mph and on braking, but I felt he was punishing his tyres too much and could not keep up that sort of pace.

'Sure enough, he had to waste valuable time changing them early on and had shot his bolt. Taruffi, whom I rated highly in sports cars and who had loads of local knowledge, took up the Ferrari challenge but we managed to build up an advantage over him. By about half distance, we were averaging 115mph before we took to the mountains again. By Rome, we were 27 minutes ahead of the record time to there.

'In spite of a brake locking which put us in a ditch on the Raticosa Pass, we still feared Taruffi – though in fact he had retired by then. Jenks said in *Motor Sport* that in the Futa and Raticosa mountains, I was working "like a maniac"! On the final fast 300km section to Brescia, we were touching 177mph and taking off on hump bridges, and flying for 50 yards. We averaged 123mph over the final Cremona/Mantua/Brescia stretch.

'For Le Mans, I was paired with Fangio who had a fantastic dice early on with Castellotti in a Ferrari and particularly Mike [Hawthorn] in a Jaguar D-type. By the early hours, we had a three-lap lead and then the powers-that-be in Stuttgart decided to withdraw the team as it was Levegh's 300SLR which had crashed into the crowd. I strongly disagreed with this at the time and still do.

'In those days the TT took place at Dundrod, near Belfast. The circuit was narrow and bumpy, and considered pretty dangerous. Sadly there were a number of fatal accidents, but I liked the challenge. This time American John Fitch and I shared a car and we were up against Fangio in another 300SLR and Hawthorn. I had built up a one-minute lead after 29 laps and then had a tyre burst which ripped away a load of rear bodywork and delayed me in the pits. Fitch took over but was losing out to Hawthorn's team mate, Titterington, who was a local man and had taken over their D-type. After six laps, I was back in the car and began to haul in Mike, especially when it began to rain. After two hours, I was back in the lead, which I lost again when I had to pit for tyres and fuel. I managed to catch the Jag once more and won the TT for the third time.

'The World Sports Car Championship all depended on the final round, the amazing Targa Florio on the 40-mile road course in Sicily which climbs from sea level to 3500ft. For this crucial final event for the 300SLR, I chose Pete Collins to drive with me. He had started in 500s like me and impressed a lot of people with his TT drive in an Aston.

'After three laps I had a lead of something like five minutes, then lost the car on the mud from a recent rainstorm. I thought I was going over the precipice and considered bailing out. It turned out to be only a ten-foot drop and, with help from some locals, I managed to get back on the road. I lost eight minutes and we were now fourth. Pete put in a tremendous drive and then I managed to go quicker and quicker. We finally won by four minutes from Fangio and, by finishing first and second, Mercedes won the Championship. These events proved just how tough the 300SLR was and, if you have great reliability, what you can achieve.'

Clockwise from above
Fangio and Moss finished just inches apart at the Nürburgring; winning the Mille Miglia has to be Sir Stirling's most famous triumph; the 300SLR was a faithful friend and a win at Le Mans, where Fangio is seen pitting as darkness falls, would have given Moss Grand Slam of sports car classics.

2 Maserati 250F

'First of all, the Maser 250F was a beautiful car to look at. But even more important, it was a beautifully balanced, very stable and predictable machine. If only it had been more reliable!

'I did 44 races in four years with various examples of the 250F. Of those, I won 15 times, was second three times and finished third seven times, but retired on no less than 13 occasions.

'In the early part of the 1950s, I had persevered with being patriotic and trying to drive British cars. But in those days our cars just weren't up to it and I had a succession of disasters. When Mercedes announced they were returning to Grand Prix racing, and bearing in mind their pre-war record, we approached Alfred Neubauer, the Team Manager, about me joining their line-up. However, he said I needed more experience in single-seaters at the top level and then he would consider me for 1955. He advised Ken Gregory, my manager, that we should buy a Maserati, for example, and show what I was made of.

'This we did because it was good advice. I insisted that Maserati, when they were building the car, fitted the throttle pedal on the right, instead of the traditional Italian central position, and altered the seating position to have more of a rake as I preferred to drive with straight arms rather than to be crouched over the wheel. Neither of my requests went down well at headquarters. In fact, Alf Francis, my mechanic, who spent some time at the factory, worked through the night and cut and re-welded a chassis tube so that the bulkhead could be moved back about six inches. Then, the next morning, Fantuzzi the body man came in and wrapped the body around the revised tubular framework.

'So, in 1954 I ran my own 250F with Alf as my mechanic, assisted by Tony Robinson. I managed to finish third in my first GP with the car. At the British GP, I was lying second with 10 laps to go when transmission problems put me out. For the German GP, I managed to be quickest in first practice and record a time eight seconds faster than Ascari's lap record. As a result, Ugolini [Maserati Team Manager] offered me a place in the works team. My rebuilt engine lasted two laps. By the Swiss GP, I was effectively leading the works team but had to retire again. The Italian GP was heart-breaking as I was leading until 12 laps

from the end when the engine lost all its oil.

'However, I had proved myself and Neubauer had noticed. He offered me a Mercedes works drive for 1955, and I continued to run my 250F for myself in more minor events and for several other drivers.

'When Mercedes pulled out at the end of 1955, I found myself with a difficult decision. Should I choose one of the up-and-coming yet unproven British teams – BRM, Vanwall or Connaught – or go back to Masers. My head ruled and I rejoined the Italian team as their number one driver for 1956.

'The 250F had been developed further during 1955 and was somewhat more reliable in '56. I managed to win in Monaco, where I led from flag to flag, and at Monza, which was nice in front of the team's home crowd. With a second at the Nürburgring and a shared third – in those days you could swap drivers during a race – at Spa, I finished as runner-up in the World Championship for the second successive year.

'In spite of their unreliability, I have very fond memories of the 250F.'

Left
Moss drove his own 250F in 1954 to prove his capabilities in Grand Prix cars – and he did so to such effect that he ended the season as number-one driver for the works team.

Above and left
Stirling did 44 races in four years with various examples of the 250F: he won 15 times, came second three times and finished third seven times – but retired on 13 occasions!

Below
Moss chats to his British rival, Mike Hawthorn, at Crystal Palace, with ace mechanic Alf Francis on their left. Hawthorn won the main race in Stirling's 250F.

Right
For the Targa Florio, Porsche fitted an experimental 2-litre engine to give more torque round the twisty, undulating course. Moss was paired with BRM driver Graham Hill.

Right
Moss loved the 'David and Goliath' challenge of taking on larger-engined Ferraris – especially after his unfortunate run-in with Enzo Ferrari early in his career.

3 **Porsche RS60**

'I suppose it is my competitive nature but I like nothing more than being David taking on Goliath. This was the situation I enjoyed on several occasions with the little RS60 and RS61 Porsches. After my run-in with Enzo Ferrari early in my career, it always gave me a special pleasure to beat his cars, especially when they had larger engines!

'For the 1961 Targa Florio, Porsche fitted an experimental 2-litre engine, rather than their more usual 1.7, so we would have more torque round the twisty, undulating course. Ten laps equated to about 450 miles and around 7000 bends! For this race I was paired with Graham Hill, who was then making a name for himself in the BRM Formula One team. He was an excellent team mate because he did exactly as he was told and didn't try and prove anything. He was utterly reliable and very solid.

'In practice, I managed to break my own lap record by 26 seconds. The Ferraris, in spite of their 2.4 and 3-litre engines, were three minutes slower.

'After the first lap I led from Jo Bonnier in another 2-litre Porsche. When I handed over to Graham, we led by one-and-three-quarter minutes from Jo, with the first Ferrari nearly two minutes down the road. Sports car specialist Olivier Gendebien then took over this Ferrari and drove very well to take second spot and then the lead. Delayed by a longish pit stop, I was now second by a minute but had a stop in hand. I managed to regain the lead and, with a lap to go, was a minute up.

'Then with just four miles to go – would you believe it – the bloody transmission seized. It was such a tragedy. The car really suited the amazing Targa Florio course and was beautifully balanced. It still hurts to have lost that one so close to home – the flag was virtually in sight!'

Below
Beautifully balanced RS60 was ideally suited to the Targa Florio course – but a seized transmission finished the car's chances of success only four miles from the end.

4 Maserati 300S

'It is hardly surprising that I liked the 300S. In 1956, when I joined the Maserati works team, I raced a 300S on eight occasions. Result? Seven wins, one retirement. If only the 250F could have been so reliable!

'The statistics are very confusing, but I actually drove the 300S in 15 races between 1956 and 1958. It is complicated because in 1956 I used two to win the Nürburgring 1000Kms, having taken over the example driven by my team mates, Taruffi and Schell. At Rabelov in Sweden, I again drove two cars that year but neither got me to the finish – one caught fire in the pits and the brakes failed on the second!

'In 1957 I started the Buenos Aires 1000Kms in a 450S Maserati but the transmission broke so I took over the Behra/Menditéguy 300S. I reckon this was one of my best races ever and wrote in my diary: "This was my greatest drive."

'The circuit was an "interesting" one. Some 6.3 miles in length, its straight doubled back on itself so, in effect, there was a two-way traffic system with the cars going each way at around 160mph. I was sharing a new 4.5-litre V8 450S sports racer with Fangio. By the 30th lap, I was in the lead by over two minutes and then I handed over to Juan who lapped all bar the second-placed Ferrari. However, the car started to give trouble and the gearbox packed up on the 57th lap.

'It was not until the 65th lap that the 300S of my team mates Jean Behra and Carlos Menditéguy was called in and given to me. I then set about the Ferraris, having inherited fourth position. I found it much easier to drive the 3-litre on the limit on this bumpy, fast track and made the quickest laps of the race in the smaller car. By 88 laps, I was up to second but could not quite catch the leading Ferrari and was 80 seconds adrift at the end. I had thoroughly enjoyed myself!

'I was still racing Maserati sports cars in '57 but mainly had the 450S model. Then, in 1958, I was officially driving for Aston Martin in sports car events, but drove a 300S on four occasions when Astons were not competing. The last time was not a very happy event because this was the infamous occasion when a Dane called Gunnar Carlsson used weaving tactics to stop me passing.

'Although the 300S never quite repeated its successes of 1956, I have very good memories of a car I could really throw around – the sports car equivalent of the 250F – which was really well balanced with a chassis far better than that of any contemporary Ferrari.'

Below
Maserati 300S victory in 1956 Nürburgring 1000Kms was actually won using two cars – Moss having taken over the example driven by team mates Taruffi and Schell.

Right and below
'I have very good memories of a car I could really throw around – the sports car equivalent of the 250F – but with a chassis far better than any contemporary Ferrari's.' In Denmark, local driver Gunnar Carlsson used all sorts of nefarious tactics to stop Moss passing, including weaving!

Above
In 1960 and '61 Moss clocked
up successive victories in the
Tourist Trophy at Goodwood
in Ferrari's iconic 250GT SWB
– these being his sixth and
seventh wins in the TT.

Below
Moss drove the Dick
Wilkins/Rob Walker 250 GT
at the rather light-hearted
Nassau Speed Week in
both 1960 and '61.

5 Ferrari 250GT SWB

'Balance seems to be the common denominator with all these cars.
It is not just a question of power, reliability or outright grip. Balance
inspires confidence and enables you to take a car to the limit, again
and again.

'I first drove a 250GT in the 1960 Tourist Trophy – a race I had
already won five times – and with the Ferrari I managed to make it six,
and four on the trot. My main opposition came from Roy [Salvadori] in a
DB4GT Aston. The classic TT had been reduced in duration from six
to three hours, co-drivers could be dispensed with and the big hairy
sports racers barred, which was a shame as they were more exciting
to drive. With only GT cars eligible, the Ferrari was a good mount and
delivered on the day. Being a closed car with a radio, I could also hear
the BBC commentary on the race, which was a weird sensation!

'I then won a minor event at Brands before taking several wins
at the annual Nassau Speed Week jamboree.

'In 1961 I drove a new Competizione model and our first event was
Le Mans, where I was to share the car with Graham Hill. We drove
under the North American Racing Team [NART] banner – a very
disorganised set-up. Graham and I had a great time, though. We were
not contenders for outright honours, or should not have been, but
by nightfall we led the GT class by at least four laps and were third
overall. However, some idiot had failed to remove the standard, roadgoing radiator fan. Unable to stand the continual high revs, a blade
flew off and chopped through a hose. We would probably have finished
second overall – in a GT car!

'My final major event in the 250GT was the annual TT at Goodwood.
Here I had stiff opposition from Mike Parkes in an identical car. Parkes
was impressive and very quick. The race was down to balancing speed
with tyre wear. My experience told and, in trying to keep up with me, he
wore out his tyres faster and had to make one more pit stop than me.
This meant that, in the end, I had a fairly easy seventh victory.'

6 Cooper F1

'For 1958, I had signed with Tony Vandervell to drive his Vanwalls but they decided not to contest the season-opening Argentine GP, which had been confirmed at short notice. I had already made a verbal agreement with Rob Walker to drive for him in Formula One and Two in events for which I was not committed to Vanwall. As a result, Rob offered me his little 2-litre Cooper for this race.

'As the current formula then allowed engines of up to 2½ litres, the Cooper was clearly going to be underpowered and I would not stand much chance, but it was better than no ride at all. Also, the little Cooper had certain advantages going for it. Firstly, for 1958 race distances and duration had been shortened. In addition, AvGas was substituted for the alcohol-based fuels and this was more economical. All these factors combined to reduce pit stops and made it possible to build a smaller, lighter and therefore more nimble car.

'The rear-engined Cooper, most importantly, was very different from the traditional front-engined racers that had dominated Grand Prix racing since the war. So I was delighted to take up Rob's offer and had nothing to lose. I also always enjoyed being the underdog with a challenge to tackle.

'As is now history, the Cooper and I came up trumps. The bigger, heavier, more powerful cars had to stop for fuel and tyres, and we managed to run with sufficient fuel to do the whole race. The tyres were another matter, though. Alf Francis, who had now joined Rob's team, and I managed to fool everyone into thinking I was going to stop for fresh rubber – and when they realised I wasn't going to, they had left it too late to make a real push. Meanwhile, I'd got down to the breaker strip between the rubber tread and the canvas. Those last laps were pretty stressful but I made it home and clocked up Cooper's first GP victory.

'I drove a number of Coopers over the next four years and thoroughly enjoyed them. They were basic but could be thrown around with great confidence, knowing they would not bite. I had a lot of fun with them and, of course, everyone else gradually adopted the rear-engined layout.'

Maserati Tipo 60/61

'Always known as the Birdcage Maser, they were fabulous. With their extraordinary construction of hundreds of small tubes, they were very light and thus very nimble. Their steering was really good and exceptionally light, and with Dunlop disc brakes they were extremely effective. The engines produced good power with tremendous torque.

'In conditions of secrecy I tested the prototype at Monza straight after the Monaco GP in May 1959. I noted in my diary it had "five speeds & very light ... time 61.3 secs!" I was immediately impressed and knew it was going to be good, providing it was reliable.

'Initially it had been fitted with a 2-litre engine but for 1960 this was increased to 2.8 litres, the engine producing 250bhp. After a rather fraught win in the Cuban GP in Havana, when the Camoradi team fitted over-hard tyres, the seat came adrift and the exhaust system dismantled itself, we headed for Sebring and the 12-hour race. By three-quarters distance my co-driver, Dan Gurney, and I had built up a good lead before the transmission gave up.

'At the Nürburgring the conditions were pretty horrible with rain and mist, which suited Dan and me. We were able to really enjoy the Birdcage and, despite having to play catch-up several times, took the win, my third in succession there.

'My next drive was at Sebring with Graham Hill in March 1961. I had asked before the start and been assured that the battery was fully charged. Flag dropped. Ran across the road. Flat bloody battery. Took six minutes to get it started. I was last. After two hours I was second – then the exhaust system fell apart. Such a shame. Lovely car that was great to drive but let down by poor preparation.'

Below
Birdcage Maserati suffered a series of misfortunes at Sebring: a flat battery and self-destructing exhaust system were among the casualties of poor preparation.

8 Aston Martin DBR1

'The DBR Astons first appeared in 1957 and were a much more serious racing car than the DB3Ss which preceded them. The new models were of spaceframe construction, and the DBR1 had a 3-litre engine while the DBR2 used a 284bhp 3.7-litre power unit. I had been impressed with the new Aston while I was driving Maserati sports racers in 1957 – and particularly when Tony Brooks and Noel Cunningham-Reid won the Nürburgring 1000Kms event which proved the cars were quick and strong. Any machine that could stand over 600 miles of the twisting, undulating, bumpy 'Ring had to be good.

'So I signed up to drive Astons for 1958 and 1959. Our first outing was the 12-Hours at Sebring, another rough track. I was paired with Tony Brooks, who I consider one of the most under-rated drivers of all time. I led and gained a lap on Salvadori's sister car and Mike Hawthorn's Ferrari. When a tyre blew, I lost three minutes – almost a lap. Tony took over and when he handed the car back to me we were a lap down on Mike. I had virtually caught him when the gearbox damn well broke. The boxes were the worst part of the Astons and horrible to use, which I thought amazing when you think that one of the David Brown group's main products was transmissions.

'The Targa Florio went badly for us but I did manage to break my own lap record, set in the 300SLR. At the Nürburgring I was paired with Jack Brabham, who was having his first drive for the team. It was not the ideal circuit on which to start. Not surprisingly, he was off the pace and I had to do most of the driving, and play catch-up twice. We won but it had taken an enormous amount out of me.

'Le Mans went badly for us and the whole team retired, my engine breaking after I had led. The TT was too easy as Ferrari did not enter, and I won from Tony.

'For 1959, David Brown was more intent on winning Le Mans than the World Sports Car Championship. So, the team was not going to enter the 1000Kms at the Nürburgring – until I persuaded them to lend me a car, if I paid the expenses: I must have been mad! I chose Jack Fairman as a good steady co-driver. During his stint he was pushed off the circuit and lost time, but I loved this sort of challenge and put in one of my best drives to catch the Ferraris and take the flag.

'At Le Mans the engine let us down again, but at least the team

finished first and second, which meant Aston Martin was now leading the Championship. All depended on the TT at Goodwood. Roy Salvadori and I were sharing and we had the lead until the car very dramatically caught fire during a pit stop. That was that. I was put into the second-placed Aston of Shelby and Fairman with a job to do. It took some doing but I managed to catch the leading Porsche which, being lighter, required less stops for tyres, and Astons won the Championship which was a very good conclusion to a great relationship. The trusty DBR1 had enabled me to put in some of my best drives ever and so I have great memories of this car.'

Left above and below
Despite ironic transmission troubles – David Brown's background was in gearboxes – Moss fondly recalls that the Aston Martin DBR1 gave him some of his 'best drives ever'.

9 Ferguson P99

'And now for something completely different. The Ferguson was quite revolutionary because, of course, it was a four-wheel-drive Grand Prix car. The man behind this was Tony Rolt, who had been a very fine driver and my team mate at Jaguar, for whom he won Le Mans in 1953, and had driven for Rob Walker before me. So Ferguson built and prepared the car, and Rob entered it for them.

'Jack Fairman debuted it at Silverstone and then drove it at the British Grand Prix at Aintree in 1961. The weather was appalling. That was the season when the Ferraris were better prepared for the new 1½-litre formula and had a load more power than the Climax-powered cars, such as the Lotus 18 I was driving for Rob. When I had to retire with brake trouble, I took over the Fergie.

'In the damp conditions it was fantastic, although it took some learning as the technique was completely different. I have never driven a car that did things so well but was so difficult to cope with. You balance a normal racer on the throttle, but with the Ferguson you just put the power on and drive it through the bend.

'Earlier on, Jack had suffered from misfiring and had pitted. He had to be push-started to get him going again. While the stewards were debating whether the car should be disqualified, I took it over and began circulating rapidly. As a result of that, Ferrari and Cooper protested and I was brought in as I had not practised in the Ferguson. A great shame.

'I drove the car once later that season, in the Gold Cup at Oulton Park. Again it was slippery, which played into our hands. I started gently to preserve the transmission but then started passing cars on the outside. It was just amazing and I won easily, even with the track drying. Fascinating machine which posed a new challenge, which I relished.'

Left from top
The four-wheel-drive
Ferguson arrived in Formula
One a shade too late, for the
writing was already on the
wall for front-engined cars.
In damp conditions, though,
it was quite unbeatable.

»

10 OSCA MT4

'I raced the OSCA just once, in 1954, but I rate the car very highly. At that time I had never been to America but very much wanted to because, to me, the States seemed to have everything – you could get coloured nylon stockings in Belgium because they came from America!

'Briggs Cunningham called up and asked if I would like to drive at Sebring. I thought, "Fantastic!" He entered his OSCA MT4, which I co-drove with Bill Lloyd. Jaguar had declined to enter a car, so I was delighted to accept his offer. I really loved the OSCA, which I described in my diary at the time as "a little beauty" and it handled really nicely.

'We were up against the works Lancias driven by Fangio, Ascari, Villoresi and Taruffi, plus the factory Astons, the Cunninghams and a load of private Ferraris and such like. We had just 1452cc. It was a really rough circuit and the weather was bad, which really helped us because the worse the weather was the more it helps (a) a small car and (b) myself!

'Gradually many of the big cars fell by the wayside, but the OSCA was losing its brakes so I was putting it sideways to slow it down. Suddenly, my God, we had won. It was incredible, absolutely incredible.

'I am so fond of the OSCA, I own one today and thoroughly enjoy racing it. A real little jewel.'

Top and right
Stirling loved his winning 1954 stint in an OSCA – which he called 'a little beauty' – so much, he eventually bought one. And, 45 years after that initial drive, he took part in the 2009 Le Mans Legend race.

Top ten WORST RACING CARS

Moss drove some great machines – but he gave it his all in some real lemons too. Here he nominates the worst 10 cars he had the misfortune to race
Interview by Philip Porter

Below
Original BRM V16 didn't work properly and suffered numerous embarrassing failures. Moss found it a fascinating exercise but hated it as a racing car.

1 V16 BRM

'Dreadful car. Without doubt, the worst car I ever drove.

'The V16 was a very interesting car, technically, but a completely unacceptable racing car. Incredibly good brakes, lovely gearbox, tremendous amount of power, but no torque. There were seven universal joints, I think, in the steering. So, you had a tremendous amount of backlash from it. It really was just a bad car. You had a centrifugal blower which wasn't good. I spent a lot of time out at Monza, supposedly testing, but had very little mileage in it.

'If something went wrong, it took them about two days to strip it down. Amazingly complex.

'The workmanship and everything was superb. To have an engine that would go to 12,000rpm was amazing but having a centrifugal blower was a bad principle from the start, in my opinion. Now, of course, 12,000 revs is nothing. Add in the chaotic organisation that BRM suffered from in those days, plus the odd behaviour of Raymond Mays, and it is not difficult to see why the BRM was a bad joke for many years.'

Maserati 450S Berlinetta

'Only the V16 BRM was more horrible! Frank Costin, who had done good work with designing the bodies of the Vanwall GP car and Lister sports racers, had been commissioned to design a closed coupé body on a Maser 450S chassis for the 1957 Le Mans race. Most unfortunately, the Italian bodybuilder put it together in far too much of a hurry and only loosely followed his plans. The detailing was dreadful and it was actually slower than the open car, which was crazy. A high maximum speed is everything at Le Mans with its Mulsanne Straight of over two miles in length.

'No thought had been given to the driver and it was hot and cramped with poor visibility. Fangio wisely decided to drive an open 450S, leaving me and Harry Schell to battle with Le Monstre, as the French called it.

'In practice, we cured the jammed throttle – someone had left a spanner in the engine! The wipers lifted off the screen at high speed, smeared the screen as we slowed down and lost contact with the glass again as we accelerated. At the start, it wouldn't! I was third for a while but not enjoying myself. It started smoking and vibrating, then an oil pipe and finally the back axle put it and us out of our misery.'

Maserati 350S

'The 300S was a lovely, sweet-handling car but struggled to keep up with the more powerful Jaguar D-types and V12 Ferraris. So, for the 1956 Mille Miglia, Maserati hastily cobbled together the 350S. It was based on the chassis from what would be known as the 450S and a highly modified V8 production engine.

'Two days before the race there were 22 mechanics still working on my car to get it ready in time. Jenks and I took the new car and a 300S to the Raticosa Pass and compared them over a timed section. The 350S was quicker but far less pleasant to drive. It wandered badly at 145mph with the nose lifting and it understeered, which was useful for slowing the car, but then I could not convert that to oversteer mid-corner to get the car set up for the next straight.

'I had little confidence in either the car or our chances of finishing. In the race we lasted as far as the long descent into Rome, losing control on some oil and coming to rest on the edge of a 300-foot drop. We were very lucky.

'This was another example of a car thrown together at the last minute, in a panic and without the benefit of any proper testing. It was a pig of a car!'

Above
1955 Mille Miglia win was hard to follow, but 350S made 1956 event memorable for the wrong reasons.

Below Fat Maser was built for 'Monzanapolis'. Moss crashed it on the banking at 170mph.

Eldorado Maserati

'Someone came up with the idea of running American Indianapolis cars against the European racers. The first time it was run, at Monza in 1957, all the European teams, apart from Ecurie Ecosse, who were tempted by the money, boycotted it. The 'Race of Two Worlds' was run again in 1958.

'The man behind the Italian Eldorado Ice Cream company went to Masers and asked them to build a car and for me to drive it. I had some fun in practice winding up the Yanks.

'In the race, I was going round at over 170mph with this bloody thing about a metre under the top of the banking. Suddenly the steering broke and so the car struck the Armco on the lip of the banking and I knocked over three great barrier posts and bent a fair section of the railing.

'Two tyres burst, I lost a wheel and it spun into the infield. I closed my eyes because I thought I was going to die. It just spun down and stopped in a load of dust and heat. Damn thing nearly killed me – not one of my favourites!'

5 Cooper-Alta

'The early fifties, 1952-1953, were strewn with unsuccessful British attempts at building a British Grand Prix challenger so that I could remain true to my patriotic principles. You have to remember that the war was still very fresh in everyone's memories and patriotism meant a lot more than it does today. Today it only really impacts on sport for most people but then the whole future had depended on fighting the common enemy together.

'Driving a foreign car was not acceptable to the public and was seen as very unpatriotic. I was persuaded to become involved with a project designed by John 'Autocar' Cooper, so known to distinguish him from John Cooper of the Cooper Car Company who, confusingly, were also involved as they supplied chassis parts and bodywork. Ray Martin, who had been running my Kieft 500 very successfully, would build the car, assisted by Alf Francis. The engine was to be a four-cylinder Alta which Alf had experience of at HWM.

'It was a disaster from start to finish really. When the engine arrived, it was larger than the mock-up and modifying the chassis ruined the steering geometry. When it was put on wheels, the front suspension collapsed. Oil leaked on to the rear drums from the diff, and so on and so on. After a few dismal races, I said enough was enough. Not a happy experience.'

Above
Cooper-Alta looked a dream, but helped Moss believe that Brits couldn't build a decent GP car: next attempt not much better!

Above
ERA G-Type frightened the horses but not much else and only finished three out of eight races with Moss.

6 ERA G-type

'Pre-war the ERAs had been very successful in the Voiturette classes. Leslie Johnson purchased the remains of the concern after the war and his first Chief Engineer, Prof Eberan von Eberhorst of Auto Union fame, was then replaced by a young engineer called David Hodkin. Johnson convinced me that Hodkin was a genius!

'Eberhorst believed in the principle of chassis construction by two large parallel tubes. Hodkin evolved this a step further with the tubes being formed by rolled magnesium to give an oval cross-section, these being joined by four cross-members. The engine was the familiar Bristol one that all sorts of people were using at that time. To get the lowest possible centre of gravity, the engine was dry-sumped and the driver's seat offset so he sat alongside the prop-shaft. This was all clothed in a rather wide body – because of the offset driving position – that was pretty ugly.

'I did eight races in the G-type. It failed to finish five times, and was third, fourth and fifth but all were minor events. It hardly frightened the Ferraris and Maseratis!'

Below
Lotus 18 in famous 1961 Monaco winning run, with side panels removed to cool the intrepid pilot: 'When it wasn't trying to kill me!'

Maserati Tipo 63

'Built like the front-engined Tipo 60 and 61, the 63 was a rear-engined Birdcage. It was as horrible as the front-engined cars were nice. It seems Maserati produced exceptionally good cars or real horrors!

'I only drove this horror once and then only briefly. Graham Hill and I were to drive a front-engined Tipo 61 at Sebring in the classic 12-Hours event in 1961. As I mentioned elsewhere, it began badly for us when I found the battery flat as I jumped in at the start. I recovered a lap and a half and was in second place. Then Graham had the manifold break which burnt his feet and nearly gassed him.

'I then took over the rear-engined Tipo 63 that Masten Gregory and 'Lucky' Casner had been driving but was soon in with a loose wheel. Went out again and 15 minutes later the rear suspension failed. That brief acquaintance was quite enough, thank you.'

Cooper-Alta Mark II

'Another well-intentioned project during my patriotic era. After the debacle of the Cooper-Alta and my decision to can it, we needed a replacement and fast. This creation was built in 11 days, believe it or not. We used the Alta engine from the first car because it was giving a very useful amount of power. This was inserted in one of Cooper's own chassis, or that was the idea. However, it would not fit with the pre-selector gearbox we wanted to use.

'Alf built a modified chassis and it was ready for the Nürburgring in just 11 days. I finished sixth, which was encouraging, and in France a week later I was third on aggregate, but these were relatively minor events. I did one Grand Prix, the Italian, and we were now using nitro in the fuel which gave us prodigious amounts of power but did not improve the health of anyone nearby! With all this power, it ripped off treads. I finished 13th.

'Although the Mark II was better, it convinced me there was no-one in Britain who could build me a competitive Grand Prix car.'

Above
Slipping Alta power into a Cooper chassis sounded a good plan – but even nitro couldn't help it.

Lotus 18

'The Lotus 18 alternated between giving me the opportunity to take some of my greatest wins ... and trying to kill me!

'I never enjoyed Lotuses in the same way I did the Coopers. They may not have been so clever as Chapman's devices but they were strong, didn't fall to bits around you and were predictable. The Lotus 18 was their first successful GP car and it was quick but it needed a lot of concentration and care.

'I won the company's first Grand Prix, at Monaco in 1960, but then had a massive accident at Spa when a wheel fell off. I also won the United States GP that year and then beat the more powerful Ferraris at Monaco in '61 when we famously removed the side panels. Finally, in upgraded 18/21 form, I managed to thwart them again at the Nürburgring. So the car brought me two of my finest victories but I never enjoyed driving them.'

Leonard MG

'The little Leonard was not unpleasant; it was just under-powered and gutless. It was a pretty car which Lionel Leonard had created by fitting a body which was a copy of a period Ferrari on a Cooper chassis with an MG engine. According to Doug Nye, it would later inspire the AC Ace which much later evolved into the AC Cobra. So this very un-exciting little car led to a seriously exciting one – eventually.

'I did just two races in this thing at Oulton Park in 1954, finishing third in my heat of the British Empire Trophy race, and was classified seventh in the final with a sick engine. Perhaps the least exciting car I ever drove!'

Above
Can you see what it is yet? Leonard MG was 'gutless' but may have inspired the Tojeiro, which led to the Ace, whence came the Cobra.

Susie Moss
AN IDEAL WIFE

Behind every great man there is usually a great woman,
and this is certainly true in Sir Stirling's case. Susie Moss
explains why her marriage works so well...
Words: Philip Porter

In 1959, en route to Australia, Stirling stopped off in Hong Kong...

Stirling Moss: 'I was then married to my first wife and I called up someone at the Rootes Group, and I said, "Listen, I am going to Hong Kong; I have never been there. Can you tell me the name of somebody I can speak to who knows about local stuff because you can get suits made there for a tenner or whatever."

'I rang the guy and he wasn't there and a lady answered and said, "Look, I am his PA, can I help you?" I explained and she invited me round. Susie was there, aged 5, along with her sister. Their mother then invited me to pop in next time I was in Hong Kong.'

Philip Porter: Susie, what are your earliest memories of Stirling?
Susie Moss: 'Being very daunted, being a small girl, being very young when he wasn't impressed with small girls. Going around this very famous house in Hong Kong and managing to get myself stuck in a high chair – my mother wasn't impressed and he was even less impressed! I always loved those, they were irresistible, you pulled down the front and… stuck! Those are my first memories of him. Scary.'

PP: How was he introduced? As a famous racing driver?
SuM: 'I don't honestly remember but he must have been very famous because I was under very, very strict instructions to behave very well!'

PP: Did he come out to Hong Kong each year?
SuM: 'I think there were a few years when he didn't. He never stayed with us originally but then he used to come and stay with us in the apartment. My memories of him then are that he was very heavily into dancing. He loved the Cha-Cha and he used to do the Cha-Cha up and down the sitting room carpet. He was lovely and I remember we got to be really good friends.'

PP: How old were you?
SuM: 'Sixteen and doing shorthand lessons and working at an advertising agency in the afternoons. He used to take me to my shorthand lessons. It was better because by then my sister had moved out, so he had her bedroom. When we were young she would move into my bedroom so he could have her bedroom, which wasn't ideal but she was always besotted with him.'

PP: What is the difference in age between you and your sister?
SuM: 'She is three years older. We had so much fun. Stirling loved shopping. He would take me to my shorthand lessons and then he would pick me up in the evening from the ad agency and we would go shopping. He was dating my sister and anything else gorgeous but it was very cool because he was driving a Mustang. Did I love that car! He would take me to my girlfriends and everywhere else in the Mustang.'

PP: Did you like cars anyway or did that one just appeal?
SuM: 'It was a very charismatic car of the period, you had *Bullitt* and *A Man and A Woman* – that whole thing was done in a Mustang, which he said was absolutely ridiculous but how romantic, just lovely. He told me that one day I would get some taste!

'I remember him getting me to school on time, which was lovely because my father always got me there late. So that was very nice when he came to stay.'

PP: Is that because Stirling is so precise about time or because he drove faster than your father?
SuM: 'Both. Stirling was staying with us when my parents dropped the bombshell that daddy was taking early retirement and we were coming

back to live in the UK. In those days repatriation was to be celebrated… but not for me. I was devastated.'

'Whilst I had visited England and Europe on our leaves my home was in the Far East as was my heart, all my friends, the colonial lifestyle and temperatures that I had grown up with. And that is where Stirling, my pal, came in, spending lots of time trying to make me believe my world hadn't come to an end and that there was a lot to look forward to on the other side of the wide water. Forty something years later I have to say he was right.'

'He would sit with me in the bedroom and say, "You will be all right," and, "London is the centre of the world," and, "I will make sure you are happy in London." He was lovely and my first night in London he took me out to dinner.'

SM: 'And a friend's wife called me a dirty old man!'
SuM: 'He was very sweet and he was very kind but I wasn't a mainliner. There was one girl he was very keen on. That was when he dumped all of us! We were just very good friends.'

PP: What period are we in now?
SuM: 'Going into the 1970s, I suppose, early '70s. I was the 'pass the peas lady'. He used to call me up at work and say, "I haven't seen you for such a long time; we must get together," and then he would say, "What are you doing tonight?" I fell for it every time. And it would turn out to be a dinner and he must have had a fight with the lady of the time, so there would have been nobody to pass the peas – there was a blank space at the table. I was aware of that, but it was OK. We were good friends, so you could do that.

'We didn't go out seriously till later. I used to go and clean the properties with him. I would have to go on the back of his scooter with my dustpan and my bucket and broom. We used to go out on the Vespa and he would go and empty the meters and I would go and clean the common parts. If I did a nice job, then he used to take me to dinner. He nearly didn't buy me dinner once when I lost the top of the broom.'

PP: As you were going along?
SuM: 'Yes! I lost it on a roundabout and he was not amused at all. He thought that was very shabby. We had a lot of fun.'

PP: Presumably it gradually got more serious?
SuM: 'Yes, and the interesting thing was that everybody could see something that I couldn't see, even from the time I was way much younger. Friends of mine would say, "You are not going to marry him, are you?" I would say, "Well why would I marry him? Of course not." For years and years and years. And I had a boyfriend who said, "You're going to marry him; I don't like him."

'It is very interesting because I never thought we would have a relationship like that. Other people could see something that I wasn't looking at.'

PP: When did you get married?
SuM: '1980. I don't think he was exclusive to me until about the day before we got married. One didn't ask questions like that. We were together from the time he asked if I wanted to try and have a baby. Then we were an item and he said, "Would you come and live here," and I said, "No," which he was probably glad about.

'He always said he didn't want any more children and I used to say, "Well, that is fine because I will never marry you. I might never have any children in my whole life but I won't marry somebody who says I can't have children." He was always very worried about people trying

'The worst day of my life would be if I woke up and he wasn't there… I wouldn't have anything to wake up for.'

Left and above right
While all about us are divorces and acrimonious splits Sir Stirling and Lady Moss have made a tremendous success of their relationship and their marriage. And while some of its elements many not suit the PC brigade there is much to learn here.

to get married to him. Again, I was very safe. It probably aggravated him that I didn't want to marry him."

PP: Did that influence the situation because you weren't keen?
SuM: 'It might have. We did have a kind of stumbling block where I got a bit miffed with his lifestyle. I just said to him, "That is fine. Don't ask me anything. I won't ask you what you do. Don't ask me what I do. If you want to see me seven days a week, then you ask me, otherwise you see me when you see me." He didn't like that at all; he thought that was very unfair. It was after that he said, "Well, if you want a baby, if we can agree to only one... I can't see any point in getting married if we don't have a child, because we are happy as we are but if you want to go ahead and try, try."

'So we tried; we had fun trying and then I thought I had flu and there was Elliott. So we got married as per the deal. I did have a contingency programme in case he changed his mind! Being pregnant wasn't any different; we just went on doing everything: wallpapering walls and painting ceilings and stuff.'

PP: Did he actually propose?
SuM: 'He did. It was lovely and in a club that we used to love, called the Wellington Club. I remember he said I could have anything I wanted [to eat] which was either a good thing or a bad thing because the last time he had said I could have anything I wanted he dumped me! This time he said I could even have snails and garlic, and I thought I don't know if this is going well or badly, but I didn't have the snails and he did ask if I would marry him. I said to him, "Would you rather I said yes or no?"
SM: 'Stupid question!'
SuM: 'I don't think he was sure at the time but he said he would prefer that I say, "yes."
SM: 'Of course I was sure.'

**PP: 'So he had to do the whole thing with my father, with me and my mother sitting in the kitchen getting the giggles. That was that. Not that many months later we were married. It was a lot of fun. That was just when he had gone back to racing [Audi touring cars]. So everything was happening at the same time.'

PP: That must have been stressful?
SuM: 'Thank God I wasn't any younger. Suddenly I am a pregnant lady, I am a married lady, I am a married lady with two houses and suddenly a very visual married lady with people watching me. He has gone back to motor racing and that is a whole other world. There are two dogs, two houses, a bump, racing and a famous husband. I think quite a few of his friends weren't that convinced that I was the right animal. It was interesting. I was very happy. I think it was probably quite daunting at the time.'

PP: What has it been like being married to a famous person?
SuM: 'Lovely! He is lovely. He is much easier now than the person I married.'

PP: He is mellowing?
SuM: 'Yes. A lot of his friends say that I have mellowed him. I haven't done anything to him. It is just time. Time has worn him down, not me. It's lovely. You marry whom you marry. I married the him that he is and he is the person that I love very much. You can't be surprised that somebody who is as successful as him has a certain kind of disposition. I think it must be very difficult if you marry somebody who is not famous or not hugely successful who suddenly becomes that way but that wasn't the case.'

PP: You knew what to expect?
SuM: 'Yes.'

'If I want to give all my time and look after him that is because I want to. It is my choice. I do it because I love him'

Left, above and top right
Stirling, Susie and son Elliott meet bronze Stirling at Mallory Park circuit; Stirling and Susie spend nearly all their time together; Susie with the author of this feature, Philip Porter.

PP: You have always been very supportive. Do you see that as your role?

SuM: 'Yes, that is what I do. I am his wife and his workmate but then I am incredibly lucky because look at all the lovely people I meet. Being with Stirling everybody says, "Oh you are really nice; you walk around and talk to everybody." It's lovely talking to everybody. If I just walked around the supermarket on my own and started talking to everybody, they would have me locked up! Because I am Stirling's wife, they think, "Oh, she's a nice lady." I meet lovely people and I love everybody who loves him, so that is easy for me.'

PP: You are incredibly unselfish.

SuM: 'I have never thought of it that way. I am just lucky.'

PP: Living in the colonies, were you brought up with traditional values?

SuM: 'Very much so. It was very colonial at that time. Dressing up on Sundays and, you know, the gloves to church and all that sort of thing. I am not unhappy with that.'

PP: Was it a male dominated, chauvinist environment?

SuM: 'Yes, but isn't that the right way? Some women would probably run me over for that. I am his wife and wives do cooking and ironing. All right, maybe I have got two jobs because I also work with him, but that is my job to look after work and a family.'

PP: So you have no time for feminists?

SuM: 'If that is the way they want to live, that is fine, but I think they are missing quite a lot by not saying, "I love you; let me do that for you."

'The one thing I would say is it is mine to give, not his to take. It is no man's to take! If I want to give all my time, devotion and enthusiasm and look after him and wash every cup and dish, that is because I want to do that. It is my choice. If he would ever turn round and say, "That is your job; you do it," I think I would get a lot more feminist about the whole thing. I do it because I love

him and I love what I do and I love our son and our home and everything. But that is why I do it, not because somebody says that you have to do that.'

PP: You are hopefully aware that everyone thinks you are the most perfect wife in the world?

SuM: 'He would laugh at that. I don't think that I am that easy to live with. I am just so very lucky. I am lucky I have got friends.'

PP: It is amazing you share so much.

SuM: 'Times change things and it changed a lot when our son Elliott got older and then I could be freer. Before that Stirling was more independent; he would do much more travelling without me. He used to travel with a good friend and go to the Grands Prix and stuff like that. He was quite happy to leave me at home. With the death of his friend and with Elliott getting older that changed. So, after that, I started doing everything with him. We started doing rallies together.'

PP: That is extraordinary. Stirling is so competitive – surely it is a recipe for the end of any marriage?

SuM: 'No! We did well. He drives me out of some mistakes but then he makes some when he doesn't listen to me. There was a wonderful bit in a video of me going, "Hard left, hard left," and he is not listening. I am then going, "OK, now left." We have great fun with that and sometimes when he is backing off I say, "Go for it, go for it. This doesn't look difficult, nothing in the road book – go!" We had fun.'

PP: It all seems idyllic.

SuM: 'It is, but don't think that we don't fight. We do. The worst day of my life would be if I woke up and he wasn't there. When you are cross with each other you just remember what would be the worst day in your life. If he wasn't there when I woke up, I wouldn't have anything to wake up for.' △

MOSS·THE *Designer*

With an analytical, ever-inquisitive mind which loves to solve problems, Sir Stirling could have forged a quite different career
Words and photography: Philip Porter

'I like things to be functional. I like things that are efficient.' Stirling is driven by a strong sense of style, allied to the fact that he is always in a hurry, always packing as much as he can into every day, every hour, every minute. Hence the ongoing quest for efficiency. He loves innovation, almost for its own sake.

If he had not made a career of motor racing, he could well have ended up as a designer. Function and form are high on his list of priorities. Beautiful women have been an integral part of his life since his teens. Architecture has also fascinated him and he has designed several houses. Clothes have always been important and he has his own, very specific requirements and style. Gadgets are one of his passions.

The true competitor is always looking for ways to beat the opposition, and part of that is seeking a legitimate advantage, often involving creative solutions. Stirling applies the same principles to many other aspects of life. He does not passively accept an item and live with its shortcomings. To him, that is too irksome and a challenge, so he applies himself to a solution. He is a great lateral thinker.

He says: 'I used to go to Hong Kong frequently and I'd design my own briefcase or shoulder bag. On one side I'd have a place for a razor and on the other a file, a portable recorder or whatever. In Hong Kong you could get those things made very cheaply and very well. That isn't the case now.

'When I buy luggage, I modify it to suit what I want. For example, I fit a series of plastic boxes inside. I put my shirts in one and it keeps them all the way they should be. The ergonomic design of so many things is so bad.'

In many ways Moss was way ahead of his time, and only in some areas has the world caught up. Quite a few of his solutions and ideas are now commonplace and may not sound exceptional, but they were in their time. There is something of the eccentric inventor in him and much of the boy with his toys. He gets a lot of satisfaction out of his

Opposite, clockwise from top left
Anyone for a cuppa? Boiling water is literally on tap, while neatness and gadgety abound throughout Stirling's house. Now, as back in the 1960s, labour-saving kit means dining chez Moss is quite an experience, and down in the garage a sliding library-style storage system keeps essentials tidy.

creative wheezes, but one should never forget that Moss fundamental – the search to save a few more seconds so he can pack that little extra achievement into every day.

There is also much clear, logical thought behind his solutions, and an open mind. He is always on the lookout for the latest innovation that he can use or maybe adapt to some other requirement. For instance, several of the more upmarket motor manufacturers, such as Mercedes and Jaguar, now have keyless ignition and unlocking systems. One simply carries a gadget in one's pocket that the car recognises.

Stirling wishes for a similar set-up for his house: 'I believe that you should be able to carry something that would tell the house it is you when you arrive. That is the way your front door should operate; it shouldn't be left just to cars.

'At the moment no lock company has ever done it and it doesn't seem as though they are even trying, but that is one idea I would like to see happen because it is such a rudimentary thing to me. You would use the locks you have got now and just modify them. I don't see why you have got to fiddle with the lock because at night you come back and it is dark and you can't find the keyhole. It would be an easy thing to do and I would love to do it.'

So, how does he keep abreast of the latest ideas and products? 'I am very lucky in that Susie enjoys going into hardware stores. We will go into a shop in America and look around and enjoy it.' Is Stirling quite sure that Susie enjoys hardware stores? 'She really does! It's amazing. She will come in with me and is quite happy. She is as happy as she is going into a … well, I can't get her to go into a clothes shop!'

Would Stirling like to have been a designer? 'Yes! I planned the layout for this house as I wanted it. I enjoy modifying things to the way I want them. That is the point really.' If all his labour-saving devices, futuristic notions and beloved gadgets ever enable him to have sufficient time, he might just launch a radical selection of cutting-edge products from the Stirling Moss Designer Range!

In discussion

Unlike today's over rehearsed media savvy racers Sir Stirling is a man who speaks from the heart and shoots from the hip... and long may it remain so
Words and photography: Philip Porter

Philip Porter: 'Most successful people are, or were, very blinkered. Some people can handle that, keep it in perspective and still remain sporting and pleasant human beings but others seem to be so focused that they are not very pleasant people at all.'

Stirling Moss: 'I have always tried to be as nice as I can with fans because I think fans are very, very important. They pay for us to enjoy our sport. That is flattering. I therefore like to do as much as I can. There are times when they are a pain in the arse – of course there are – such as when you go to a motor show and people are continually pestering you. I can understand famous people find that an annoyance, but it is something I try to handle properly... if I can.'

PP: 'There was an interesting piece which I quoted in one of our books about Hawthorn and Collins who really were just

out for a good time and didn't really give much of a stuff about the fans or being professional. You, however, were thinking of your future and the fact that when you retired you would need those people still to be supportive of you. You would be in business, you said, and they would potentially be your customers. So you thought ahead about that in the late '50s whereas they just thought about the next pint or the next race.'

SM: 'You see when you get to 32 and you have no training in anything and you know nothing about anything, there are two things that you can be – one is an estate agent and the other is a politician. Those are the only two things where you don't need to know about anything at all. Hence, the fact that you can take a stupid woman who can't drive and make her Minister of Transport. When she screws that up you move

her on to something else like the Ministry of Employment. That is what politics is.'

PP: 'Have you ever thought of going into politics?'

SM: 'No, actually I haven't. As I get older, it interests me more. I wouldn't think of going into it at all now; I am too old anyway. I would find it very frustrating, I think. I haven't got the time to be a dictator but that is what I would like to be. Politics amazes me: the older I get the more I understand about it. All these things they are talking about now are just the tip of the iceberg, I reckon.'

PP: 'In a sense you almost became an estate agent with your rental property in London?'

SM: 'That is because it was the other alternative, wasn't it!'

PP: 'You could have been a designer? An architect?'

SM: 'No, I couldn't. I couldn't be a dentist like my father, you see, because I couldn't qualify. I hadn't got sufficient qualifications, knowledge and understanding. I couldn't be an architect you see.'

PP: 'Not qualified no, but perhaps a designer, although maybe that concept didn't really exist in those days. I guess Terence Conran almost invented that.'

SM: 'I find it very frustrating. I suppose if I was in the business I would know where to go to get a prototype done of this or that. Really, I have never had the time to follow it up because I have always got something else that is pressing at the time.'

Above
Sir Stirling never failed to keep good company - David Brown and Carroll Shelby make particularly good companions.

PP: 'Time, again!'

SM: 'The one thing you can't make.'

PP: 'You try to with labour-saving and clever devices.'

SM: 'Yes.'

PP: 'You like modern technology and embrace it.'

SM: 'The modern technology that I can handle, I love! I use a laptop computer but I don't know enough about it. I find it frustrating because of my short-comings. It is rather like getting into a car and finding they have put a limit on the throttle. Really, it does annoy me but I can't do anything about it. If I was much younger, I could because I am sure there are kids of nine or ten who know a hell of a lot more than I do. I used to do logarithms and all that sort of stuff, but they wouldn't even know what it is [today]. I am really sorry that computers didn't come a bit earlier when I was a bit younger. I have a great respect for them.

'I had every intention and a belief that I would certainly be racing when I was 50. I was very fit. I think I was just about at my zenith when I had the crash when I was 32. I would have thought that I would have had at least another 10 to 15 years. That was my intention.

'It was my hobby you see. I was very fit when I was racing, I think I was as fit as they are today, but I never did any training at all. I was racing every week and water skiing and so on, doing all the sort of things that one did do. It is quite a different situation today.

'As to the racing driver's life of today, my quality of life when I raced was ten times better than Lewis's now. We are talking just enjoyment of things. I know what his life is like because I know that at 10 o'clock he is going to land with a helicopter, at 10.05 he will be with the press, at 10.20 with the TV, at 10.35 he will be with me doing this... that is the sort of life.'

PP: 'Was money ever the motivation for you?'

SM: 'No, no. I certainly would look and see what the prize money was as soon as I got to a race, certainly I would. But I came from a middle-class family; my father was a dentist, a successful one. I was striking hard bargains if I could. Leslie Johnson was the one that said I should get £1000 a year from BP, which was a lot then. But I would get in somebody's car and critique it and I wouldn't expect to be paid for that.'

PP: 'Do you think you would have made it in racing if your father had been a dustman?'

SM: 'No. I think, if karts had been around I might have done. There is no doubt that a dustman, at that time, wouldn't have been able to afford a 500 and I wouldn't have been show jumping to make the money to pay for it. So, from that point of view, no.'

PP: 'Maybe if you had started with a humble saloon and built your way up, somebody would have spotted you? That is the only alternative scenario. I wonder if you would have had the determination, if it was important enough for you?'

SM: 'Yes, because it wasn't the racing particularly, it was the success. The success is what feeds you. The ego and pride are fed on success, not on the actual thing you are doing. It comes in many ways. The one thing I regret very much is I never did Indianapolis. It just wasn't feasible in my time to do it. It would have been stupid. I would have loved to have done it because of all the bullshit, you know.

'When I think back and I think of all the different types of racing I did, it was a tremendous, tremendous opportunity, really: when roads and racing were dangerous and it was exciting. That is why I am very lucky because if I had

Above
While Sir Stirling was certainly successful with the ladies you have to be rather confident to get away with his favourite line: 'Will you stay for breakfast?'

come along now – it is a very mundane life by comparison to my life.'

PP: 'You enjoyed the acclaim?'

SM: 'Oh yes, most certainly. It is very nice for people to come up and recognise you and have you sign an autograph and all that, particularly when you are young and fewer people do it because you are not well known around the world.'

PP: 'Your Christian name was very distinctive.'

SM: 'That was thanks to dad that I was called Stirling because my mother wanted to call me Hamish. Hamish, doesn't ring at all, really!

'Another thing that helped me a lot was the fact that racing was in its infancy after the war. There were no established stars to beat. I was very young, so I was one of the younger ones. I was fairly successful and they hadn't got much to write about in racing; there weren't races all over the place and they were all over here to start with, so I got quite a lot of press. Then I went abroad and they followed me… I came at a very good time.'

PP: 'Quite a few people would have been older because they had been in the war and also quite a number of them went into motor racing because they craved the action and risking their lives. They may not have been that good but they missed the excitement and the adrenalin. They would have been less serious competition.'

SM: 'There were a few people out there who had raced before the war, but not many. I think Peter Walker and Tony Rolt had but not many.'

PP: 'How would you chat-up a female back in the 1950s?'

SM: 'If they came around to the house and had a drink or something, or if we had been out at a party or something, I think one of my favourite lines was, "Will you stay for breakfast?"'

PP: 'What would you chat about when you were dancing?'

SM: 'I think one would probably talk about all sorts of things. I am a fairly facetious person and try to keep it tongue in cheek.'

PP: 'Presumably, not motor racing?'

SM: 'Only if they wanted to. Motor racing is the bait, the glamorous lifestyle. If they happened to ask questions, because some girls were very keen, obviously one would, but generally no.'

PP: 'Did you read newspapers and keep abreast of what was happening in the world?'

SM: 'I did keep abreast of films and shows and things like that.'

PP: 'You enjoyed dancing. Would that be traditional ballroom type?'

SM: 'Ballroom and Cha-Cha and things like that. Jive wasn't that popular, more the Twist and all those sort of things – Foxtrot.'

PP: 'Did you tell awful jokes in those days?'

SM: 'I think I must have done. It is my style, I think!'

PP: 'Food and wine are important to you today.'

SM: 'I didn't drink until I was 32. Only when I married my second wife and she said to me, "Oh come on, loosen up and have a drink". Now it costs me more money to drink wine than it ever did because I know a bit about it and the more you know the less interesting things like Liebfraumilch are. I have always been keen on food, but I was never a wine drinker, at all. I only drink white wine now. I have half a bottle a day.'

PP: 'What sort of food do you like and have your tastes changed?'

SM: 'I don't think they have. I have always liked roast beef, I have always liked shepherd's pie.'

PP: 'So very traditional British?'

SM: 'Yea, roast beef, roast duck, roast chicken. Yes, I suppose you are right. I like seafood. We go Japanese now and again. I like French cooking providing it is moderately well done, à point, medium. The French are very inclined to under cook food and I don't like undercooked food.'

PP: 'Susie has been an extraordinary partner, companion, wife, hasn't she?'

Above
It is unlikely that Sir Stirling would ever have been a racing driver if his father had not been a successful dentist, yet the young Moss worked hard to make things happen financially.

SM: 'Unbelievable. Do you know we have been married nearly 30 years. In all that time not one thing in this house has gone to a laundry! We don't even know if there is a laundry. She does the sheets, she does all my clothes, all her own clothes, the whole lot. Then you reckon she has got six floors which she keeps clean. Then you realise that she cooks the meals. Then you realise that she is in the office answering letters. She helps me. Everywhere I go, she comes. It wouldn't work with many wives; I know it wouldn't with either of my other two. My first wife couldn't take the strain of racing, which I understand. The second one I wouldn't want with me anyway. It is an extraordinary thing how it has worked.'

PP: 'You are incredibly lucky.'

SM: 'I am incredibly lucky, because I am incredibly difficult, as well. To have somebody who is prepared to accept my dreadful shortcomings, and I am not easy… I have had a fantastic life and Susie has been terrific.'

PP: 'I suppose to use a pun, you are a very 'driven' person, which I guess makes you a little bit tricky to live with?'

SM: 'I am sure. I am always on the go, which must not be easy but Susie is the same; she is just as bad. This morning we woke up very early and I said, "I am going downstairs because I am going to do my workout". So I came down and took her up a drink and then, my God, she is down here working. I was in the plumbers' merchant's at 7am. So quite a good morning. No time wasted today. It is amazing how much you can get done!'

PP: 'Have you ever worked out how many hours you work a week?'

SM: 'Usually, I am in the office by 7am to 7.30am and I am always in here at that time of night. We don't stop for lunch – a sandwich, or something similar, is all we have and Saturdays and Sundays are just the same, really. We work a full week. What is so good you see is that Susie enjoys doing a lot of things and I do. There is always something on. 'Movement is tranquillity' – that is what you have got to remember.'

Scooters

He's a demon on two wheels as well as four – but it's the lure of functionality, ease of parking and more than a little style which have made Stirling a long-time scooter fan
Words and photography: Philip Porter

Stirling is famous for his scooters, and it could well be said that he helped to popularise this Italian invention in the UK. He had his first Vespa around 1952 and found them to be the ideal transport on which to get around, whether it be at a circuit or in central London. Always one to favour lateral thinking, he saw the new scooters not only as practical but as something of a fashion statement as well. Moss was never a Mod, however: he says the only mods he has been into are technical ones and the only rockers he has known are to be found inside engines!

Talking of lateral thinking, he has fallen off a few two-wheelers in his time. Indeed, such moments have added to the many breaks and injuries which have been suffered by his much-abused self. Luckily he has always been immensely fit, and that maltreated body has historically recovered remarkably quickly.

There was no better example of this than when he crashed heavily at Spa in 1960, breaking both legs and crushing three vertebrae in his back. He was walking 23 days later, riding a bike (with a nurse on the handlebars) five days after that and in a racing car in another week!

Of his scooter history, he says: 'The Vespa was the first model I owned. The problem was that the gearchange was on the handlebars.' But why scooters? 'I felt they were easier to ride than a motorbike because you step through them and you can carry a lot of stuff where your feet are. They are good to get through traffic, easy to park and you have a windscreen. I went to my sister's wedding on a scooter in a morning coat! It's just much easier to get around.'

Initially he had a wide variety of Vespas, but he then tried something different. 'I rode a Triumph scooter that was an automatic, which was very good – but then, of course, the company stopped building them. Eventually I want back to Vespas, which are now made by Piaggio.

'Then, a while ago, I skidded on some diesel going under the bridge at Waterloo. I fell off and had the bike on top of me, and broke my pelvis. So I told Susie I was going to get a scooter with three wheels. Mine has two at the back and one at the front, so if I get on to oil, I spin rather than go over. The one I have now has a full windscreen and I have had it tuned. It gives about the same performance as a taxi, and can go at up to 35mph.'

'So, today you race taxis?' I ask. 'Actually, I think they would just about beat me. My scooter is only 50cc. It's a Honda Gyro. They are not imported to the UK. A particular company in Biggin Hill, Bat Motorcycles, decided to bring in 100 of them, so I bought one.

'Some time ago I got a ticket from the police which cost me £75. At the time I had a 100cc Honda but I took it in for repair and I was lent a smaller one that was only 50cc. I went on the motorway spur by Shepherd's Bush in London. The cops pulled me over and said: "This is too small for this road," and I had to pay a £75 fine. So now I have had my own scooter over-bored; it is actually 53cc. I am waiting to be pinched, but legally I can go on there now.

'A moped is hard work, a scooter isn't. A scooter is self-propelled rather than human-powered, whereas a moped is a bit of both. I don't like motorbikes really – they are rather heavy. I found that with a scooter I could put a ramp up into the back of my Honda van, ride up it, then go over to Silverstone, unload and just go around on the scooter.

'Living in London it is very convenient; I don't own any road vehicle other than the Honda van. The scooter is a most convenient mode of transport – particularly this present model because it gives me some protection.

'Ken Livingstone [former London Mayor] charged me road tax, so I went to see him. He admitted that I shouldn't be paying; he was after Reliant Robins and all that stuff. He said: "I can't give you an exemption; we'd have to get the law changed." Well, a year later the law changed.

'The only pleasure I get from driving on the road in London these days is on my scooter, because I can find a place to park and can get through the traffic easily.'

Opposite
Casual, in overalls or suited and booted, style king Moss was a fan from the earliest days of scootering. He could be spied at race tracks and on the street astride the latest Italian – and British – machinery.

THE PERSONAL ORGANISER

house

He was quite the young man about town back in the day – and, five decades on, Moss still lives in the gadget-laden bachelor pad he built on a London bomb site

Words: Philip Porter Photography: Abigail Humphries

A mark of how extraordinary Moss' Mayfair mews was in the 1960s is that it has stood the test of time. As with all good design and original thought, it is as fresh and contemporary today as it was when it was built back in 1962. We now have computers, digital sound and images, home cinemas and other such hi-tech gadgetry as a matter of course... but who else, other than Stirling Moss, has a table that descends from the kitchen to the floor below, a tray that carries items from an office on one storey to an office on another, and the means to run a temperature-controlled bath from any other room? Heath Robinson would have been proud of Stirling!

So, completely untrained and using a mix of common sense, observation, practical thought and innovation, Stirling set to work in 1960/'61 designing a new house from scratch. He had bought the site in the heart of London's Mayfair: a German bomb had thoughtfully cleared a small area for him to build what he referred to as his 'dream house' – _Ideal Home_ meets _Grand Designs_!

Stirling recalls: 'I would start by asking: "What do I need? How many bedrooms? How many bathrooms? Where should they be? Do I want to be on my own on one side or whatever?" I would lay it out on a plan and then I would look at the plan and think, well it would be nice if I did this and that, and I put in the windows where I wanted them and that sort of stuff, and it just happened.'

He sacked his first architect, who probably refused to contemplate so much fresh thinking. You can just imagine it: 'Oh, we don't do things like that. No one has ever done that before, so we can't. You want to do what?'

Stirling drove the project, commissioning a female architect to translate his ideas into reality. The house was a very 'technical' design, for it involved going down as well as up. Today people are building virtual estates beneath their London mansions, but back in the early 1960s it was less

usual to have your guest bedroom underground. The Moss dwelling is narrow, dictated of course by the width of the small site between two existing buildings. There is a hall leading from the central front door, with a garage on each side. One garage extends to the back of the plot, and features a great deal of storage beyond the area put aside for a car. Stirling has a series of metal storage racks on rails so they can be slid together normally and parted only for access, rather like a library book storage system. At the rear of the other garage is his office, the nerve centre.

A spiral staircase makes maximum use of space: it descends to the guest area and ascends to the first floor, where there is a large sitting room, a small 'snug' off this with TV and video, plus Lady Susie's office. Climbing again reaches the large kitchen with another relaxation area (not that either Moss does much of that), and the dining room. Above is the master bedroom, walk-in wardrobes with motorised shutters and the main bathroom, and yet another floor houses a second guest room and balcony.

Stirling had to go to Germany for the large sitting room windows, which open either conventionally or tilt at the top – more prevalent today, but radical in the early 1960s. He says: 'In Germany there are some incredible hinges; they do have wonderful ironmongery.' Stirling is a real hardware enthusiast, with an almost religious zeal.

Like the man himself, the house is small, neat, precise and very well organised. It has to be, because of the lack of space in this prime central London spot. He laughs: 'With my home, there is a place for everything and everything is in its place. I try to keep it that way.'

He continues: 'If I want to run the bath, I can push a button on any floor and it actuates three electronically controlled hydraulic valves, which are what radiators have. One of them closes – that is the waste – and the other two are on hot and cold and they open. So, now the water is coming out hot and cold. It then goes through one of those bi-metal jobs, so

Above At work and at play, Moss abode reflects Stirling's love of neat functionality. Spiral stairs make most of site's limited space and curl up six floors from basement, passing first-floor lounge.
Left Family room extends off the kitchen on the second floor.
Right Master bedroom, with its own terrace, is on the third floor.

'Convenience and time saving are common themes, but comfort has its place chez Moss, too'

you can't scald yourself, so I set the temperature. I always have the same; I can change it but not remotely. So then the bath runs for five minutes, 20 seconds, or whatever, and there it is, ready to go. That to me is very convenient. I don't have to swill the water round and I don't have to watch out for it to overflow. That is very convenient.

'I also have a radio-controlled garage door, which these days is very ordinary but back in 1962 it wasn't. Then I have got the descending table, which is a device whereby you can send a meal down from one floor – in this case, the kitchen – to the floor below on a sort of table at which you can sit. That is pretty convenient as well. It is actually a Ratcliffe tailgate [as used on lorries]; that is all. It is the way it has been put in that matters.

'What else have I got? Instant boiling water, which is the most beneficial thing as well as the most used, and which anybody in the house can get hold of. Again, this is really quite common now, but it is undoubtedly my most used item. If I am going to make a cup of coffee or tea, I do not need to boil a kettle.' So convenience and time saving are common themes, but comfort has its place as well. 'I have heated toilet seats, so if you are a long time on the loo, you

Clockwise from top left
Guest room houses just some of Stirling's library, while the basement guest sitting room features yet more motor sport memorabilia – as well as trophy door stop! Motorised roller shutters hide clothes neatly away, and ground floor toilet has graffiti wallpaper and heated seat.

have got the pleasure of that!'

We now live in an age when energy conservation and a Green agenda increasingly dominate our lives. Can Stirling relate to all this? 'Efficiency, yes. The Green thing I don't fully understand, but I like to design things that are functional. If I ever build another house, I have got quite a lot of ideas for it. Now solar panels and so on are very common, which they weren't a few years ago. Quite a lot of things like that, which I think are very good.'

Is Moss tempted to update the London house? 'That is interesting because I have been wondering if I should do a makeover. Quite honestly, there are things one could always change, but it is difficult here in this place because I have got the circular staircase, which is established.

'When I look around my home, I have got most of the conveniences I would want. I have got my boiling hot water out of the tap, I have got the special running bath. I can't think of that many other things.'

Has Stirling Moss, designer, run out of ideas? Or was he actually so far ahead of his time five decades ago that there remains little else conceivable for him to tax his ever-inventive, questioning, problem-solving mind?

Holidays

When you are a workaholic, time off comes with its own set of challenges. Which begs the question, how is it Sir Stirling can be such a fan of ocean cruises – perhaps the most relaxing of all holiday pursuits...?
Words and photography: Philip Porter

'A holiday for us now is quite different to how it was in my racing days. We used to take our holidays on our way to and from various events. Now, I enjoy cruising because you get on and I can fiddle around with designs, or I can read a book, or I can meet people and talk to them, or work out, or whatever. The people look after you so well. You wouldn't believe the service on a good line. Having said that, I couldn't do too many. Even if I were free, I wouldn't squeeze in many more.'

Knowing his lack of patience and his dynamism, I am amazed Stirling likes something as gentle and laid back as a cruise. 'So am I!' is his response when I put that to him. It certainly appears, on the face of it, to be totally out of character. Is it one place he can relax?

'It isn't relaxation – at least in the way most people would understand it. To me, it is doing something different. Doing something different is a relaxation, that is the point.'

During his racing career, Moss used to go to the south of France quite a lot but, not surprisingly, he did not sit for long on the beach. He would be water-skiing most of the time, or visiting night clubs – often several in an evening. He was even known to frequent casinos, though he has always been far too shrewd to have anything more than what would be termed a flutter.

His favourite holiday spot was Nassau, to such an extent that he purchased some land and built a house there. 'Nassau always had something to do with chasing girls; I had quite an active life out there, you know!

'Nassau was also a Sterling area at that time. This is why I went on holiday there, because at one time you were allowed to obtain only £50 foreign currency a year. I had got to know people there and the weather was good, and I thought it was a nice place.'

Even at 80, Moss cannot sit down for long and, to this day, you would never find him on a beach. 'I have got to a situation where I can enjoy a book, which for me is remarkable. In my whole life I have maybe read ten books. That was because I was hoping they would make a film about it and I wouldn't have to bother to concentrate! I can't read fast enough; I read everything slowly. Some people can scan read and consume a book very quickly. I can't. When I read a book, it takes me a long time because I have to read every word.'

With Moss being a workaholic, you sense he feels a tinge of guilt, particularly today, about taking time off – and he is reluctant to use the 'h' word.

'It's a change, more than a holiday. I really enjoyed learning the Targa circuit or something like that. It's quite intricate, going round and round you know, once an hour for 15 hours, day after day, but it's still quite interesting. That was different and a change.'

Air travel today is desperately tedious and must drive Sir Stirling up the wall with all the hanging around, the queuing for security, then the planes sitting on hold because they have missed their slot, and so on. It is enough to drive a patient man to distraction and a waste of that most precious commodity of all – time.

'I don't enjoy the travelling. I enjoy getting there,' he says. Stirling was very much one of the first jet-setters – a rare breed in the 1950s. As his diaries prove, his schedules were amazing, and every year he must have been one of the most widely travelled individuals in the whole world. With less people flying then, it was a very different experience to today and, of course, the handful of terrorists had yet to impact on the many millions who now travel by air. 'There was much less hanging around than there is now – and when I was racing, there was very little of it.'

In those days there was a glamour about flying and a buzz of excitement, even for adrenalin junkies. But for Stirling there was a more major attraction that made the whole experience even more thrilling, enjoyable and challenging.

He met, and went out with, loads of air stewardesses! ⚠

Opposite, clockwise from top left
Skiing in Wildhaus, Switzerland; 1960, Nassau; water-skiing in the south of France; 29 May 1960, France; December 1958, in the Bahamas with Katie and Pat; showing good form out on the water; 1959 Portugal; September 1956, Stirling and Katie in the south of France.

Quicksilver

Two very different generations of Mercedes SLR, the legendary 300 and the new McLaren, tested by Sir Stirling Moss and David Coulthard
Words: Sir Stirling Moss/Ian Fraser (300SLR);
David Coulthard/David Lillywhite (McLaren)

For a few heady months in the mid-1950s, an intoxicating rumour, spread by word of mouth, by telephone, by letter and by teleprinter (the clattering predecessor of email) bombarded the sports car fraternity: Mercedes-Benz was going to put the mighty 300SLR into production for the select few to buy. The car had been so brilliantly successful in competition that its very name made the spine tingle. The thought of it as a fast road car and sports-racer was simply electrifying.

It was all a dream, a fantasy. Tall-tales start because of ignorance of the facts. And the simple fact was that the SLR was then the highest of all high-tech machines. Consumer money could not buy the expertise that made the SLR win races; and to convert it to a lower 'customer' specification would have been a nightmare of compromises.

Ironically, the SLR's iconic reputation is based on only one season's racing. But what a season! The cars finished in first place in five of the six races they entered in 1955, starting »

'The 300SLR's iconic reputation is based on only one season's racing. But what a season! The cars finished first in five of the six races entered in 1955, starting with Moss' sensational win in the Mille Miglia'

with Stirling Moss' sensational win in the Mille Miglia (possibly the greatest race success ever) on May 1 and concluding with victory in the Targa Florio on October 16 (Moss/Collins). The race they did not win was Le Mans because the cars were withdrawn after Levegh's tragic accident, in which his SLR was lethally propelled into the spectators, killing more than 80 of them.

Of course, much of Mercedes-Benz's success was due to the calibre of the team's drivers, who included Stirling Moss, Juan Manuel Fangio, Hans Hermann, Karl Kling, John Fitch and Peter Collins. But they had been attracted by the calibre of the cars.

A driver would only need to look at the SLR's specifications to realise that Mercedes was on to a racing certainty. A development of the straight-eight 2.5-litre Grand Prix engine in the W196 that swept all before it from the beginning of the 1954 season, the sports car power unit had a capacity of 2982cc, Bosch high-pressure fuel injection and a compression ratio of 9:1. Twin overhead camshafts, gear-driven from the centre of the crankshaft, mechanically opened and closed each cylinder's two valves, thus doing away with troublesome valve springs; the crankshaft was assembled in sections, using the Hirth principle, making possible one-piece connecting rods and roller bearings throughout. Cast in two sections of four to ensure greater accuracy in the walls, the alloy cylinder blocks were capped by integral cylinder heads.

With everything attached, and ready for the chassis, the engine weighed in at 517lb – the sort of thing an Olympic weightlifter could deal with. The surprise, though, was the power output. At a time when we nonchalantly expect any sort of sporting hack to deliver unto us at least 350bhp, and supercars are nudging 1000bhp, the earth-shattering 300SLR seems anaemic with 300bhp at 7500rpm and 220lb ft at 5750rpm. Barely enough for granny to take to the shops.

Or so you may think. Although I did not have the opportunity to drive the SLR on the road, 10 laps or so of the full Hockenheim long-circuit took the wraps off some of the car's abilities. Truth to tell, 300bhp can be ample when it is allied to a small car of light weight (1830lb) and superb balance. A stopwatch would have revealed a 0-100mph time of about 12 seconds had I not been restricted to 6000rpm instead of the race figure of 7500rpm and, with high gearing, a top speed of 180mph; figures not altogether dissimilar to those of my considerably more powerful, and 20 years younger, Ferrari Daytona.

The engine spluttered at low revs, especially if it had been idling for more than a couple of minutes, allowing the plugs (two per cylinder) to fuel up. Everything about the engine sang of racing. It was never happier than when the tachometer needle was storming around the white numerals on the instrument's black face. So smooth, so assured, so effortless once it got to its natural home on the action end of the crankshaft speed.

Above right
Archive pictures show Moss and Jenks on the 1955 Mille Miglia. Engine features early fuel injection.

Mercedes 300SLR
SPECIFICATIONS

Engine
2982cc, eight-cylinder, four overhead cams, 16 valves, desmodromic, dry-sump lubrication

Power
310bhp @ 7400rpm
220lb ft @ 5750rpm

Transmission
Five-speed manual rear-mounted with diff

Suspension
Front: double wishbones, torsion bars, telescopic dampers
Rear: single-pivot swing axle, torsion bars, telescopic dampers

Brakes
Finned light-alloy drum brakes all-round. Air-brake for some races

Weight
901kg (1982lb)

Performance
0-60mph 7 secs.
Top speed 186mph

And so noisy. The exhaust note was magic as the two very slightly muffled pipes, exiting just about level with the passenger on the SLR's right side, sounded as though someone had unleashed the Valkyries on a bad hair day. However, much of the cacophony originates from under the bonnet as the desmodromic gear proves that, for road cars, life is better with conventional valve springs. Desmo mechanisms have been around for almost a century and, although used in motorcycles, have not found their way into modern passenger cars because of the decibel level.

Other factors would severely cloud fantasists' vision of using an SLR to impress their friends down at the pub. Getting in and out requires a specialised and intricate technique that does not come too readily; the beautiful spaceframe – light and immensely rigid – makes for a very wide door sill; removal of the large, wood-rimmed, four-spoke steering wheel (though Moss used a three-spoke), which detaches from the hub after releasing a couple of clips, is also a necessity. You have to get your arrival in the cockpit exactly correct because the cover over the clutch and propeller shaft (running between your legs at engine speed, let me remind you) intrudes into the driver's zone, creating the need to straddle the housing with the clutch pedal on the left and the other two on the right. This slightly oddball arrangement is because the offset engine is tilted 30 degrees over to the right to reduce bonnet height and, of course, to lower the centre of gravity.

'I could drive flat-out into a bend knowing exactly which way it would go. Well, on most occasions...'

Moss on the 300SLR

Every time I get into the SLR I am staggered that it is only 3 litres. On the 1955 Mille Miglia we topped out just short of 180mph on the road, and that was when 180mph was fast.

The SLR is a large car, about the same size as the Aston Martin DB3S. Its power and strength always impress me. It is a real man's car, not a vicious one. But it's not easy, either. It is a serious sports car and you wouldn't get into it and drive it flippantly.

On the Mille Miglia the drum brakes were very good but I am glad they were not too good otherwise I would not have broken the record. At the end of the 1000-mile race the shoes had worn down to the metal but they still worked in a fashion.

The Mercedes handles very well and you can kick the tail out on tight bends, but you do have to remain mindful of the rear suspension. On road races like the Mille Miglia you have to keep things clean and avoid the rough road edges, kerbs and other hazards. My navigator [on the 1955 Mille Miglia] Denis Jenkinson helped here. With his map reading I could drive flat-out into a bend knowing exactly which way it would go. Well, on most occasions...

I can't think of any car with more history. I won the Mille Miglia, the Tourist Trophy and the Targa Florio in this SLR, and I would imagine it is probably the most valuable car in the world.

And to maintain as even a weight distribution as possible, the gearbox is mounted at the back, behind the rear axle line. The servo-boosted brakes – drums all round – are inboard front and rear to reduce unsprung weight. Suspension, by torsion bars, includes dampers which are finned for cooling to resist fade. All this is so elegant and beautiful that it's almost a pity the bodywork has to hide it from admiration.

With its long rearward voyage, I had half-expected the gear-change mechanism, positioned for right-hand use, to be a little vague and wobbly. It was neither, but the pattern proved to be odd, being the reverse of the norm: first to the left and up; second down and to the centre; third straight up from there; fourth down and to the right; top straight up. It took a mile or two to get the hang of it – and to overcome my surprise at how superbly the gears slid from slot to slot, the Porsche synchromesh ensuring easy passage. The clutch – it's a single-plate unit – did not require super-strong leg muscles and although it bit with some ferocity when engaging first from rest, it was smoothly reassuring thereafter.

As a competition car there was no point in hanging about and letting the plugs foul and the whole thing turn grumpy, so I let it bark its way around Hockenheim for a few laps, getting accustomed to the SLR's feel. And what a feel it was: it was as though it had been hewn from the solid; beautifully precise, eager, magnificently balanced and completely harmonious. To call it relaxing would be wrong but I never had concerns over what it was doing, or was about to do. Acceleration was strong, very strong, as the ultra-smooth engine wound itself up, and the handling immaculate despite the relatively early manifestation of independent, single low-

Clockwise from top left
Moss coaches Coulthard in the art of 300SLR entry; F1-style snout; V8 is set back under the screen scuttle; Coulthard more at home in SLR – panel in centre hides ICE/sat-nav.

pivot swing-axle rear suspension. Getting the braking and downward changes sorted out before the corners was essential of course, for cars like this do not tolerate drivers who are still braking as they turn in (brilliant in the SLR) any more than they forgive backing off halfway through a bend.

Without aspiring to set lap records or even drive very quickly, I nonetheless had a hugely enjoyable and spirited time in the SLR, picking up hints as to why it was the greatest sports-racing car of the post-war period. Significantly, the drivers who piloted SLRs during that epic 1955 season have, rightly, heaped praise on them ever since, expressing astonishment at their ruggedness and durability, and the ability of the team to get the best from them. Their last race, the Targa Florio in October, saw the cars leaving the road, going through walls and bumping into other competitors, but each time they returned to contention and finished first, second and fourth; battered but completely undaunted.

Unlike the dreamers of all those years ago – and knowing what I know now – I would have loathed to see any form of SLR turned into something for the masses. Its iconic status now, half a century later, ensures its immortality. Given access to the Daimler-Benz boardroom minutes it might be possible to ascertain why the company opted to abandon its competition programme on October 22.

Perhaps the accountants had discovered how costly it really was to run both Grand Prix and sports-racing programmes, so it was decided to retreat and get on with the business of making some of the most admired of road cars. Five decades later, though, the name has returned and a fantasy of sorts has become material.

So much history, legend even, to contend with. The tag of 'the greatest sports-racing car of the post-war period'. From the start, the SLR McLaren was saddled with three letters it couldn't live up to. But as a high-performance road car, I hoped it would still shine; I imagined that it would feel like an über-powered AMG SL, as sophisticated as it is powerful. But it didn't.

Why not? Because this bloody thing's a brute. It's billed as a supercar but it's more of a super-muscle-car, a modern-day Cobra that you hitch a wild ride on, if you dare.

Not that it seems that way at first, despite the aggressive Formula One-inspired snout, long bonnet, short cabin and even shorter boot. You plip the Mercedes remote control, there's a gentle kerthunk as the central locking slides open, and then you pull on the handle in the flank behind the door and watch in satisfaction as the door swings up in a semi-gullwing arc.

What's revealed is a plush, glitzy interior, packed with recognisable SLK parts, leather and aluminium. Drop in over the sill, noting that this is far, far easier to climb into than most supercars. At this point it's no real surprise to find that the seat adjusts electrically up, down, back, forward and at just about any angle on the single seat-shaped switch, and that the steering column adjusts for height electrically. You start the engine by flipping a silver cover atop the gearlever and pressing the 'Fire' button. PlayStation addicts will love it; I'm not convinced. But there's nothing remotely PlayStation about the sound effects.

Coulthard on SLR McLaren

I first encountered the SLR in a couple of photo sessions in Germany and Italy, then in a huge hall in Berlin where they built Zeppelins. In that location it looked lost.

The styling is just incredible and really underlines the sporty character of the car. The moulding of the front end is reminiscent of a Formula One car. What impresses me most of all is that all the visuals – such as the gills at the side – are not just there because they look good, they also have a technical and aerodynamic role to play.

I'd recommend the SLR to a 'normal' driver without a moment's hesitation. It offers all the important driver assistance systems to boost active safety, including ESP. Apart from which the car is superbly well balanced. It handles so well, and the performance of the brakes is really outstanding. Everything that you can take out of a racing machine which it makes sense to use on the road is already built into this model.

To get an accurate impression, you have to drive this car around town, so that's exactly what I did. And no sooner had I completed my test run around the streets of Monte Carlo than I placed an order for an SLR of my own. I opted for a silver one, which just brings out the lines of the SLR to perfection, best of all in the evening twilight on the Cote d'Azur.

I'm still a great fan of my F1 car. But it would be wonderful if I could transfer some of the creature comforts from the SLR into the cockpit of my racer...

> 'Everything you can take out of a racing car that it makes sense to use on the road is already built into this car'

A roaring SUCCESS

Sir Stirling is a household name – for the second time around, thanks to his exploits narrating the children's animated series Roary the Racing Car

Sir Stirling Moss is Britain's best known and most loved racing driver with people of a certain age, but now, thanks to his work as the narrator of the BAFTA-nominated pre-school smash hit, Roary the Racing Car, he is becoming a household name with a new generation of fans.

The series, now in its second year, presents motor racing to a pre-school audience for the first time. Set at Silver Hatch race track, the stories focus on a single-seater called Roary and his racing car friends. These include an Italian Formula One car known as Maxi, an American NASCAR saloon called Tin Top, Oriental Drift Car Drifter and a French rally and stunt car called Cici, plus Mr Carburettor – the mega-rich Italian owner of Silver Hatch.

The latest episodes, out now, feature other original characters including Loada, a transporter lorry from Eastern Europe, Breeze, a cool, lively, free-spirited Australian beach buggy, and Mama Mia, Mr Carburettor's mum. She is driven by the diligent James, a classic Aston Martin-inspired 'chauffeur' car with lots of gadgets.

Along with Sir Stirling, the popular programme includes comic genius Peter Kay, who voices the karaoke-singing mechanic Big Chris – who acts as a father figure to the cars, catchphrase 'you bend it, you mend it' – and Tin Top, as well

as the hilarious new Big Christine – Big Chris's mum.

Like Sir Stirling Moss, the series is truly British, produced at the Chapman Entertainment studios in Altrincham, Cheshire. It includes stop-frame animation, which means that each character puppet is moved 25 times for every second seen on screen. This is combined with superior CGI, which provides audiences with a real sense of speed when the cars are racing around the track. Each animator produces up to 11 seconds of footage every day, which is then used to create a 10-minute programme.

The voices of all the characters are recorded first and the animators then synchronise this with the footage. There is a huge amount of attention to detail involved which makes Roary the Racing Car a series that children and parents alike can enjoy together.

Talking from his Mayfair home, Sir Stirling Moss comments on the hit series: 'I love being involved in Roary the Racing Car. The programme is a great way for young children to learn who I am. The show is internationally recognised and provides kids with an exciting introduction into the world of motor sport, through fun storylines, fantastic songs and great humour. I have a lot of fun recording the narration and I enjoy working with Peter Kay.'

Roary is the fastest-growing pre-school boys' brand in the »

This page
Moss finally gets his hands on a single-seater again. Roary the Racing Car is introducing a whole new generation to motor sport, and Sir Stirling is very proud to do his bit.

Above
Here's where all the stop-frame action happens. That's Tin-Top, after some Dukes of Hazzard-style off-road action, Drifter, Cici – and Mr Carburettor behind the Armco.

UK (Source: Aprl NPD) and the show has now been sold to more than 110 countries worldwide with race fever gripping the imagination of children globally. The programme concept was originated by David Jenkins, who once worked at Goodwood and Brands Hatch. He came up with the original idea while watching Grand Prix racing on television with his son, then aged 18 months. His agent sent it to Chapman Entertainment, who loved it! Keith Chapman then worked on the design of the show and developed it by introducing new characters.

Keith Chapman is the originator of Bob the Builder and creator of Fifi and the Flowertots, and the company produces the Fifi and the Flowertots show. The firm was formed in 2002 by Chapman, Executive Producer and Managing Director Greg Lynn and Commercial and Financial Director Andrew Haydon, and there is a raft of future projects for a range of age groups in development.

Roary the Racing Car is consistently ranked as a top-performing programme with viewers tuning in daily to watch their favourite four-wheeled friend. Don't miss Sir Stirling Moss in all his glory each morning in Roary the Racing Car on Five's Milkshake! and Nick Jr. △

'Roary the Racing Car provides kids with an exciting introduction into the world of motor sport'

Above
Here's where all the stop-frame action happens. That's Tin-Top, after some Dukes of Hazzard-style off-road action, Drifter, Cici – and Mr Carburettor behind the Armco.

Below
Moss at the mic. He narrates the series; the characters' voices are recorded by Peter Kay and others, and the animation is added to suit.

Classic-Benz Limited
Fine Cars from Private Collections
www.classic-benz.co.uk   Tel Andrew Stansfield on 07787 182 700

We are proud to Celebrate Sir Stirling Moss's 80th Birthday and have his 1995 SL500 Milia Miglia as presented by Mercedes to him in commemoration of his Famous 1955 Milia Miglia Victory. Chassis No. 1 and with enhanced power and suspension. This car also features in Stirling's Book of his Favourite Cars!

It is also the 50th Anniversary of the Mercedes Fintail this year, we have two of the finest examples in Europe. 1962 Historic Rally 220SEb, £46k restoration, FIA papers. 1965 220b only 25k miles, Concours Winner this year.

Three of the finest R107 SL's to be found - 1989 300SL, just 1k miles from new, totally as new, unique. 1989 500SL, 3k miles, the penultimate production car, the final one in the Stuttgart Museum. 1989 500SL, 26k miles, including air conditioning, in show condition, Three incredible opportunities.

Superb original examples of the sporting E Class W124 - 1993 500E, the finest available, 1995 E220 Sportline Cabriolet, only 27k miles, 1994 E220 Cabriolet, one owner just 52k miles.

GETTING *Older*

He may be about to celebrate his 80th birthday, but Stirling Moss shows few signs of slowing down, either in his personal life or with his racing...
Words: Philip Porter
Photography: Philip Porter and Abigail Humphries

There was a wonderful feature in an American motoring magazine in 1961 which asked, 'Is Stirling Moss a human or a robot?' It featured a large diagramatic drawing of the side view of Stirling in reclined driving position, with all the human joints illustrated with cog wheels, solenoids and similar mechanical devices. The question was left open for the reader to decide. It was a wonderful spoof – though the magazine did actually receive a letter from an earnest reader demanding to know which he was: 'I think we should be told'. Amazing.

However, even Stirling Moss gets older, though he defies the process better than the majority. Of course, his career has taken its toll on his body. He's had his share of accidents though very rarely were they his fault. Usually something fell off (remember, he drove Lotuses!) or seized, or he was involved in someone else's Horlicks.

Ever the realist, he admits feeling a bit older albeit, 'from the point of view that I am not able to do anything like the amount of things I used to. I can't lift the weights I used to do. Though I do have more time because I am awake more hours, but I am not as with it as I was. I can't tick things off nearly as fast as I used to.'

However, like all of us, whatever our age, he still feels young in himself. He certainly does not feel 80. I suggest 40; he counters with 50.

'Today has been a particularly good day from my point of view. I was down at the plumbers' merchants at 7.30am picking up some stuff to give to my son before 8.00am.'

When asked why he is still working so hard, he says, 'Because I enjoy it. I am a workaholic. My father was much the same.'

Alfred Moss built up the largest group of dental practices in the UK and used to work on multiple patients at once – he would start a process on one patient, go into another room and work on another patient, then go back to the first or even

onto a third, and so on. 'He was always doodling with this or playing with that. For example, he bought some tinplate and solder and made me a suit of armour. He was always doing something like that.

'As long as I can keep my mind busy, I think retirement would be the most appalling thing.'

Moss has some firm views on this and offers sage advice to others considering kicking back their heels and taking it too easy in their advanced years.

'Don't retire! Pull out of one thing and go into another. You see, there are certain people who are so set on stopping at 60 or 65 or whatever. They say, 'Right then, I am through with this job at the post office. That is it, I am going to retire.' I think that is appalling. I think it is the most ageing moment possible. Unless you can say, 'OK I have finished with that lot, BUT now I am going to damn well do this...' Whatever it is, stamp collecting or whatever, it doesn't matter.'

Stirling respects people who work, and do an honest day's work for an honest day's pay. He does not mind if someone works slowly as long as they do not charge him for their slowness. Plumbers spring readily to mind! 'You have to pay plumbers something like £300 a day. But if he comes in and gets on with it and does a good job, great, no problem. If he comes in and does £150-worth of work and charges you £300, that does upset me.'

As to people who could work but choose not to because they are idle: 'I have no respect for them.'

Stirling's only concern about getting older is that one has less time left. When asked if it concerns him that the name of Stirling Moss stands for speed and his dynamic, jet-setting life may, inevitably, be seen to be slowing down a little bit, he immediately assumes that the question relates purely to the race track.

'Well, I like to hope that the people I race against now are mostly still slower than me anyway. Therefore, I am still competitive.'

Opposite, clockwise from top left
Moss with his tribute statue unveiled at Mallory Park in 2006; racing his C-type and a borrowed Frazer Nash Le Mans Replica at Monaco; chatting with Jodie Kidd at Goodwood; joy with Murray at Silverstone in 2008 – and 'Marilyn'!

British Grand Prix
1957
Vanwall

British Grand Prix
1955
Mercedes

RKX 991

THE COMPLETE

Master Events List
FTD = Fastest time of day
FL = Fastest lap
FTP = Fastest time in practice
PP = Pole position

1947

March
18 Harrow CC Moss Trophy Trial
Winner Cullen Trophy in BMW 328

April
9 NW London MC Inter-club Trial
Unclassified in BMW 328 (broken half-shaft)

June
28/29 JCC Eastbourne Rally
1st class award in BMW 328

September
5 Brighton Speed Trials
7th in 2-litre standard sports class in BMW 328
18 Poole Speed Trials
3rd in class in BMW 328
20 Chichester Speed Trials,
Merston Aerodrome
Unclassified

1948

May
9 Prescott Hill Climb
4th in class in Cooper-JAP 500 Mk II

June
5 Stanmer Park Hill Climb
FTD in class in Cooper-JAP 500 Mk II

July
4 Brough Aerodrome races,
1st in heat in Cooper-JAP Mk II, 1st in final
15 Bouley Bay Hill Climb, Jersey
FTD in class in Cooper JAP 500 Mk II
18 Prescott Hill Climb
FTD in class in Cooper-JAP 500 Mk II
25 Great Auclum Hill Climb
FTD in class in Cooper-JAP 500 Mk II, 2nd overall

August
6 Boscombe Speed Trials
FTD in class in Cooper-JAP 500 Mk II, 2nd overall

September
5 Brighton Speed Trials
4th in Cooper-JAP 500 Mk II
12 Prescott Hill Climb
3rd in class in Cooper-JAP 500 Mk II
18 Goodwood, 500cc race
1st in Cooper-JAP 500 Mk II
25 Shelsley Walsh Hill Climb
FTD in 750cc class in Cooper-JAP 500 Mk II

October
2 Silverstone 500cc race
Ret'd in Cooper-JAP 500 Mk II (gearbox sprocket)
9 Dunholme Lodge Aerodrome
1st in 500cc race in Cooper-JAP 500 Mk II

1949

April
19 Goodwood, 2nd Easter Handicap
1st in 500cc race in Cooper-JAP 1000 Mk III
Ret'd in Cooper-JAP 500 Mk III (piston)

May
14 British GP, Silverstone
1st in 500cc race in Cooper-JAP 500 Mk III
26 Manx Cup, Douglas, IoM
Ret'd in Cooper-JAP 1000 Mk III (magneto)
28 Blandford Hill Climb
FTD in class in Cooper-JAP 500 Mk III

June
11 Shelsley Walsh Hill Climb
2nd in 1100cc class in Cooper-JAP 1000 Mk III
25 Bo'ness Hill Climb
2nd in 1100cc class in Cooper-JAP 1000 Mk III, 4th overall

July
10 IX Circuito del Garda, Italy
3rd in heat in Cooper-JAP 1000 Mk III, 3rd in final, 1st 1100cc class
17 Reims-Gueux, Coupes des Petites Cylindrées, France
Unclassified in Cooper-JAP 1000 Mk III (chain broke)
21 Bouley Bay Hill-Climb, Jersey
2nd in 1100cc class in Cooper-JAP 1000 Mk III, 3rd FTD overall
31 Zandvoort 500cc, Netherlands
1st in Cooper-JAP 500 Mk III

August
20 BRDC Silverstone
2nd in Cooper-JAP 500 Mk III
27 Prix du Leman,
Lausanne, Switzerland
Ret'd in Cooper-JAP 1000 Mk III (engine, Gold Cup for most meritorious performance)

September
11 Prescott Hill Climb
FTD in 1100cc class in Cooper-JAP 1000 Mk III (class record)
17 Goodwood, Madgwick Cup
1st in Cooper-JAP 1000 Mk III;
Goodwood Trophy, F1 race,
ret'd in John Cooper's Cooper-JAP 1000 Mk III
24 Shelsley Walsh Hill Climb
FTD in Cooper-JAP 1000 Mk III (38.19 secs)

October
2 Brough Aerodrome races
3rd in heat 2 in Cooper-JAP 500 Mk III, 3rd in final; handicap race, ret'd (engine)

1950

April
10 Easter Goodwood, Event 1
6th in HWM; Third Easter Handicap, 2nd in HWM

16 Brands Hatch, 500cc races
Ret'd in Cooper-JAP 500 Mk IV (piston)
30 Paris GP
Ret'd in HWM (con-rod)

May
13 British GP meeting,
Silverstone, 500cc race
1st in heat & 2nd in final in Cooper-JAP 500 Mk IV
14 Prix de Mons, Belgium
6th in heat 1 & 7th in final in HWM
20 Prix de Monte Carlo, Monaco
1st in heat & 1st in final in Cooper-JAP 500 Mk IV
28 Circuit du Lac, Aix-les-Bains, France
Ret'd in HWM (car problems & SM unwell); 500cc race, ret'd in final in Cooper-JAP 500 Mk IV (engine failure)

June
11 Rome GP, Caravalla Baths, Italy
Ret'd in HWM (stub axle)
17 Goodwood, 1500cc sports cars
5th in Cooper-MG
25 Brands Hatch, 500cc races
Open Challenge, 1st in heat 1 in Cooper-JAP 500 Mk IV, 1st in final; 1st in Production Cars heat in Cooper-JAP 500 Mk IV, 1st in final; 1st in 10 Fastest Cars race

July
2 Coupe des Racers 500,
Reims, France
6th in Cooper-JAP 500 Mk IV; Coupe des Petites Cylindrées, 3rd in HWM
9 Bari GP, Italy
3rd in HWM
22 Naples GP, Posillipo, Italy
1st in heat in Cooper-JAP 500 Mk IV, ret'd in final (accident)

August
7 500 Trophy, Brands Hatch
1st heat 2 in Cooper-JAP 500 Mk IV, 2nd in final; Daily Telegraph Trophy, 1st in heat in Cooper-JAP 500 Mk IV, ret'd in final (carburettor)
12 Prix de Berne, Switzerland
Ret'd in HWM (gearbox)
26 BRDC Silverstone
9th heat 2 in HWM, 6th in final; 1st in Cooper-Norton 500 Mk V

September
10 Circuit de Mettet, Belgium
4th in heat 1 in HWM, 1st heat 2, 2nd overall on aggregate
16 RAC Tourist Trophy, Dundrod
1st in Jaguar XK120
17 Brands Hatch, 500cc races
1st heat 2 in Cooper-Norton 500 Mk V, ret'd in final (gearbox)
24 Circuit de Perigueux, France
2nd in heat 1 in HWM, 3rd in final
30 BARC Goodwood
7th in HWM; 2nd in Cooper-Norton 500 Mk V

October
7 Castle Combe

1st in HWM; 1st in heat in Cooper-Norton 500 Mk V, ret'd in final (carburettor); 1st in 2-litre sports cars in Frazer Nash Le Mans Replica; 1st in Team Handicap in Frazer Nash
15 X Circuito del Garda, Italy
Ret'd in HWM (stub axle)
24/25 Montlhéry, France
24-hour run in Jaguar XK120 with Leslie Johnson, 2,579.16 miles, average speed 107.46mph (172.93kp/h)

November
8/11 Daily Express Rally
Completed road course unpenalised in Aston Martin DB2, failed driving tests, with Lance Macklin
21/23 Montlhéry, France
record breaking in Kieft-Norton 350, with Ken Gregory & in Kieft-Norton 500 with Ken Gregory & Jack Neill

16 F1 wins

1951

February
10 Chiltern Night Trial
Unclassified in Tony Woods' Morris Minor

March
26 Lavant Cup, Goodwood
1st in HWM

April
8 Marseilles GP, France
3rd in HWM
22 San Remo GP, Ospedaletti, Italy
5th in HWM
29 Mille Miglia, Italy
Ret'd in Jaguar XK120 (accident)

May
3 500cc Luxembourg GP, Findel
Ret'd in heat 2 in Kieft Norton 500
5 BRDC International Trophy, Silverstone
6th heat 1 in HWM; 14th in final; 1-hour Production Sports Race
1st in Jaguar XK120, FL, Team Prize
13 Monza Autodrome GP, Italy
4th heat 1 in HWM, 3rd heat 2; 3rd overall
14 Whit-Monday Goodwood
9th in heat in Kieft Norton 500; 1st in final
20 Columbus Centenary GP, Genoa, Italy
Ret'd in HWM (transmission); 500cc race, ret'd in Kieft-Norton 500 (suspension cable broke)
27 Swiss GP, Bremgarten, Berne
8th in HWM

June
3 Circuit du Lac, Aix les Bains, France
1st heat 2 in HWM; 2nd in final
10 Rome GP, Baths of Caracalla, Italy

Results

4th in HWM
14 British Empire Trophy, Douglas, IoM
1st in Frazer Nash
24 Le Mans, France
Ret'd in Jaguar C-type (engine)
July
1 AVUS, Berlin, Germany
Ret'd in HWM (engine)
8 Rouen GP, Les Essarts, France
Ret'd in HWM (gearbox)
14 British GP 500cc race, Silverstone
1st in Kieft-Norton 500
15 Circuit de Mettet, Belgium
4th in HWM
22 Dutch GP, Zandvoort, Netherlands
3rd in HWM; Dutch GP 500cc race, 1st in Kieft-Norton 500
29 German GP 500cc race, Nürburgring
Ret'd in Kieft-Norton 500 (broken steering arm)
August
5 Freiburg Mountain Climb, Germany
4th F2 in HWM; 500cc class, 1st in Kieft-Norton 500
12 GP OstSchweiz, Erlen, Switzerland
ret'd in HWM (suspension)
September
2 Bari GP, Italy
Ferrari 166, DNS
8 Wakefield Trophy, Curragh, Eire
1st in HWM
15 RAC Tourist Trophy, Dundrod
1st in Jaguar C-type, FTP, Team Prize
23 Modena GP, Italy
Ret'd in HWM
29 Madgwick Cup, Goodwood
1st in HWM; Sports Car race, 1st in Jaguar C-type; 2nd September Handicap, 2nd in Jaguar C-type; 3rd September Handicap, 2nd in HWM; Daily Graphic Trophy, 5th in HWM
October
13 Winfield races, Scotland
1st in HWM
20 Brands Hatch 500cc races
1st in heat 3 in Kieft-Norton 500; DNS in final (broken gearbox); Brands Hatch Championship, 1st heat 2 in Kieft-Norton 500; 1st in final

00
World titles

1952
January
22/29 Monte Carlo Rally
2nd overall in Sunbeam-Talbot 90
February
17 Kitching Trophy Trial
7th in Harford III
March
24 Lyon-Charbonnières Rally

2nd in class in Jaguar XK120 Coupé, 15th overall
April
12 Castle Combe 500cc races
1st in heat 3 in Kieft-Norton 500; 1st in final, FL; Team Relay Race, unplaced in Frazer Nash
14 Earl of March Trophy, Goodwood
1st in Kieft-Norton 500; First Easter Handicap, 4th in Jaguar C-type
May
4 Mille Miglia
Ret'd in Jaguar C-type, with Norman Dewis
10 BRDC Silverstone 500cc
3rd in Kieft-Norton 500; Touring Car race, 1st in Jaguar Mk VII; Production Sport cars, 1st in Jaguar C-type; The Race of Champions, 1st in Jaguar XK 120
11 Brussels GP, Bois de la Cambre, Belgium
Ret'd in Kieft-Norton 500 (accident)
18 Swiss GP, Bremgarten, Berbe
HWM withdrawn (suspension failure)
22 Luxembourg GP, Findel
1st heat 2 in Kieft-Norton 500; 6th in final
25 Eifelrennen, Nürburgring, Germany
2nd in HWM; 500cc race, ret'd in Kieft-Norton 500 (rear hub sheared)
29 British Empire Trophy, Douglas, IoM
Ret'd in Kieft-Norton 500 (ignition)
June
2 Monaco GP
Disqualified in Jaguar C-type (outside assistance);
Prix de Monte Carlo, ret'd in Frazer Nash (wheel fixing)
7 Ulster Trophy, Dundrod
Ret'd in BRM V16 (engine, etc)
14/15 Le Mans 24-Hours, France
Ret'd in Jaguar C-type (overheating)
22 Belgian GP, Spa-Francorchamps
Ret'd in ERA G-type (accident)
29 Reims Sports Car race, France
1st in Jaguar C-type; Marne GP, unclassified in HWM
July
11 Alpine Rally
1st in class in Sunbeam-Talbot 90
19 British GP, Silverstone
Ret'd in ERA G-type (overheating); 500cc race, 1st in Kieft-Norton 500
20 Namur GP, Belgium
1st in heat in Kieft-Norton 500; Ret'd in final (suspension)
27 Fairwood Aerodrome, Wales
Ret'd in heat 2 in Kieft-Norton 500 (accident); F3 Invitation race, 3rd in Kieft-Norton 500
28 Prescott Hill Climb
2nd in Kieft-Norton 500
August

2 Daily Mail Trophy, Boreham
3rd ERA G-type; Sports Car race, 1st Jaguar C-type; 500cc race, 3rd in works Cooper-Norton Mk VI
4 Brands Hatch, August Sprint
2nd heat 4 in Kieft-Norton 500; 2nd in final; Daily Telegraph Trophy, 1st in heat 3 in Kieft-Norton 500; ret'd in final (engine threw rod)
5/12 Montlhéry, France
Seven day records in Jaguar XK120 Fixed Head Coupé, total 16,851.73 miles (27,119.49kms)
16 Goodwood Nine Hours
5th in Jaguar C-type
17 Dutch GP, Zandvoort
Ret'd in ERA G-type (engine); 500cc race, 1st in Cooper- Norton 500 Mk VI
23 Turnberry, Scotland
1st in heat 2 in Jaguar C-type; 1st in final;
500cc race, 1st in Cooper-Norton 500 Mk VI
31 Grenzlandring, Netherlands
3rd in Cooper-Norton 500 Mk VI
September
7 Italian GP, Monza
Ret'd in Connaught A-Type (engine)
27 Goodwood 500cc race
1st in Cooper-Norton 500 Mk VI; Sports Car race, 2nd in Jaguar C-type; Madgwick Cup F2 race, ret'd in ERA G-type (accident); Goodwood Trophy Formula Libre race 5th in ERA G-type
October
4 Castle Combe 500cc race
1st heat 1 in Cooper-Norton 500 Mk VI; 1st in final; F2 race, ret'd in ERA G-type (steering)
11 Charterhall, Scotland
2nd in Jaguar C-type; 500cc race, 2nd in Cooper-Norton 500 Mk VI; F2 race, 4th in ERA G-type
November
12/15 Daily Express Rally
13th overall & class award in Jaguar XK 120 Fixed Head Coupé
December
2 15-Countries run
In Humber Super Snipe in 3 days, 18 hours, with Leslie Johnson, John Cutts and David Humphrey

1953
January
20/27 Monte Carlo Rally
6th in Sunbeam-Talbot, with Desmond Scannell and John A. Cooper
March
Jabbeke, Belgium
Timed at 120.459mph in Sunbeam-Talbot Alpine
Montlhéry, France
Achieved lap at 116mph in Sunbeam-Talbot Alpine

April
6 Goodwood, Lavant Cup
7th in Cooper-Alta Special; Earl of March Trophy 500cc, 3rd in Cooper-Norton 500 Mk VII
26 Mille Miglia, Italy
Ret'd in Jaguar C-type, with 'Mort' Morris-Goodall (back axle)
May
9 BRDC International Trophy, Silverstone
2nd heat 1, 9th final, in Cooper-Alta Special; Production Touring Car race, 1st in Jaguar Mk VII; Sports Car race, 7th in Jaguar C-type
16 Ulster Trophy, Dundrod, NI
2nd in heat 1 in Connaught A-type; unable to start final due to gearbox problems
25 Crystal Palace, Coronation Trophy
4th in heat 1 in Cooper-Alta Special; 5th in final;
500cc race, 1st in Cooper-Norton 500 Mk VII
31 Eifelrennen, Nürburgring, Germany
6th in Cooper Alta Special; 500cc race, 1st Cooper-Norton 500 Mk VII
June
6 Dutch GP, Zandvoort
9th in Connaught A-type
13/14 Le Mans 24-Hours, France
2nd in Jaguar C-type
18 British Empire Trophy, Douglas, IoM
2nd in heat 3 in Jaguar C-type; final, 4th
28 Rouen GP, Les Essarts, France
10th in Cooper-Alta Spl
July
5 French GP, Reims-Gueux
1st in Cooper-Alta Special
10/16 Alpine Rally
Coupes des Alpes for penalty free run in Sunbeam-Talbot Alpine
18 British GP, Silverstone, 500cc race
1st in Cooper-Norton 500 Mk VII
26 Jubilee GP, Lisbon, Portugal
2nd in Jaguar C-type
August
2 German GP, Nürburgring
6th Cooper-Alta Mk II
9 Sables d'Olonnes GP, France
4th in heat 1 in Cooper-Alta Mk II; 5th in heat 2; 3rd overall on aggregate
15 Charterhall, F2 race
Ret'd in Cooper-Alta Mk II (fuel injection);
Formula Libre, ret'd in Cooper-Alta Mk II (engine); 500cc race, 1st in Cooper-Norton 500 Mk VII
22 Goodwood 9-Hours
Ret'd in Jaguar C-type (engine)
September
5 RAC Tourist Trophy, Dundrod, NI
4th in Jaguar C-type, 1st in 3-litre class
7 Italian GP, Monza

13th in Cooper-Alta Mk II
19 Crystal Palace, London Trophy
1st in heat 1 in Cooper-Alta Mk II, PP;
1st in heat 2, PP; 1st overall on
aggregate; Redex Trophy 500cc race,
2nd in heat 2 in Cooper-Norton 500 Mk
VII; final, ret'd (carburettor dropped
off)
20 Prescott Hill Climb
1st Cooper-Alta Mk II
26 Goodwood, Madgwick Cup
2nd in Cooper-Alta Mk II;
Woodcote Cup, 4th in Cooper Alta Mk II;
Goodwood Trophy, ret'd in Cooper-Alta
Mk II; 500cc race, ret'd in Cooper-
Norton 500 Mk VII (slipping clutch)
October
5 Castle Combe 500cc race
1st in heat 1 in Cooper Norton Mk VII;
Joe Fry Memorial Libre Race,
ret'd in Cooper-JAP 1100 Mk VII
(accident)

66
F1 starts

1954
January
18/25 Monte Carlo Rally
15th in Sunbeam-Talbot Alpine
March
7 Sebring 12-Hours, USA
1st in Briggs Cunningham OSCA
April
10 British Empire Trophy, Oulton Park
3rd in heat 1 in Leonard-MG; ret'd in
final (engine)
17 Goodwood, 500cc race
7th in Beart-Cooper Mk VIIA
May
9 Bordeaux GP, France
4th in Maserati 250F
15 Silverstone, BRDC International
Trophy
3rd in heat 1 in Maserati 250F; ret'd in
final (de Dion tube broke); Production
Touring Car race, 3rd Jaguar Mk VII,
PP; 500cc race, 1st in Beart-Cooper Mk
VIIA
23 Eifelrennen 500cc, Nürburgring,
Germany
1st in Beart-Cooper Mk VIIA, FL
29 Aintree '200', Formule Libre
3rd in heat 1 in Maserati 250F; 1st in
final; 500cc race,1st in Beart Cooper
Mk VIIA, FL
June
6 Rome GP, Castelfusano, Italy
6th in Maserati 250F
12/13 Le Mans 24-Hours, France
ret'd in Jaguar D-type (brakes)
20 Belgian GP, Spa-Francorchamps
3rd in Maserati 250F
July
4 Reims 12-Hours, France
Ret'd in Jaguar D-type (transmission)
9/16 Alpine Rally
Coupe des Alpes en Or for 3rd
consecutive penalty-free run, in
Sunbeam-Talbot Alpine
17 British GP, Silverstone
14th in Maserati 250F (transmission)

25 Caen GP, Le Prairie, France
2nd in Maserati 250F
August
1 German GP, Nürburgring
Ret'd in Maserati 250F (engine)
2 Daily Telegraph 500cc races, Brands
Hatch
2nd in heat 4 in Beart-Cooper Mk VIIA;
2nd in final
7 Oulton Park Gold Cup
1st in Maserati 250F; Formula Libre
race,
1st in Maserati 250F; 500cc race,
1st in Beart-Cooper Mk VIIA
15 Pescara GP, Italy
Ret'd in Maserati 250F (oil pipe)
22 Swiss GP, Bremgarten, Berne
Ret'd in Maserati 250F (oil pump)
September
5 Italian GP, Monza
10th ret'd in Maserati 250F (split oil
tank)
11 RAC Tourist Trophy, Dundrod, NI
18th in Jaguar D-type
25 Goodwood Trophy
1st in Maserati 250F; Woodcote Cup
Formula Libre,
3rd in Maserati 250F; Sports Car race,
2nd in Lister-Bristol; 500cc race,
2nd in Beart-Cooper Mk VIIA
October
2 Aintree, Daily Telegraph Trophy
1st in Maserati 250F; Formula Libre
race
1st in Maserati 250F; 500cc race
1st in Beart-Cooper Mk VIIA
10 Coupe du Salon, Montlhéry, France
1st in 1500cc class in Connaught ALSR,
7th overall
24 Spanish GP, Barcelona
Ret'd in Maserati 250F (oil system)
November
29 American Mountain Rally
Team Award in Sunbeam-Talbot Alpine

1955
January
16 Gran Premio de la Republica
Argentina (Argentinian GP)
4th with Kling & Hermann in W196
30 Gran Premio de la Ciudad de Buenos
Aires
1st in heat, 2nd overall on aggregate in
3 litre-engined W196
March
13 Sebring 12-Hours, USA
6th overall & 1st in Production Car
Class in Austin-Healey with Lance
Macklin
April
11 Goodwood Race Meeting
Sports Cars up to 1,500cc
ret'd in Beart Rodger (engine) Climax;
Chichester Cup
3rd in Maserati 250F; Richmond F1
Race
ret'd in Maserati 250F (fuel injection)
25 Bordeaux GP
4th in Maserati 250F
May
1 Mille Miglia
1st at record speed in Mercedes-Benz
300 SLR (with Denis Jenkinson
navigating)
7 BRDC International Trophy Meeting,

Silverstone, Sports Car race
Ret'd in Beart Rodger Climax; Daily
Express International Trophy,
Ret'd in Maserati 250F (engine)
22 Monaco Grand Prix
Ret'd in Mercedes-Benz W196 (engine)
29 Eifelrennen, Nürburgring, Germany
2nd in Mercedes-Benz 300SLR
June
5 Belgium Grand Prix, Spa
Francorchamps
2nd in Mercedes-Benz W196
11 Le Mans 24-Hours Race
Leading after 9 hours when 300SLRs
withdrawn by Mercedes-Benz, with
Juan Fangio
19 Dutch Grand Prix, Zandvoort
2nd in Mercedes-Benz W196
July
16 British Grand Prix, Aintree
1st in Mercedes-Benz W196
24 Civil Governor's Cup, Lisbon,
Portugal
1st in Porsche 550
August
7 Swedish Sports Car Grand Prix,
Kristianstad
2nd in Mercedes-Benz 300SLR
13 Redex Trophy, Snetterton
3rd in Maserati 250F
20 Nine-Hours Race, Goodwood
Ret'd in Porsche (accident)
27 Oulton Park
Sporting Life Trophy
5th overall & 2nd in class in Standard
8; Daily Herald Trophy
7th overall & 1st in 1,500cc class in
Connaught ALSR
September
3 Daily Telegraph Trophy, Aintree
Ret'd in Maserati 250F (engine)
11 Italian Grand Prix, Monza
Ret'd in Mercedes-Benz W196
Streamliner (transmission)
17 RAC Tourist Trophy, Dundrod,
Northern Ireland
1st in Mercedes-Benz 300SLR, with
John Fitch
24 Gold Cup, Oulton Park, England
1st in Maserati 250F
October
16 Targa Florio, Sicily
1st in Mercedes-Benz 300SLR, with
Peter Collins

1956
January
7 New Zealand GP, Ardmore
1st in Maserati 250F; Ardmore Sports
Car Handicap,
1st in Porsche 550
22 Argentine GP, Buenos Aires
Ret'd in Maserati 250F (engine)
29 Buenos Aires 1000 kms
1st in Maserati 300S, with Carlos
Menditéguy
February
5 Buenos Aires City GP, Mendoza
2nd in Maserati 250F
March
24 Sebring 12-Hours, USA
Ret'd in Aston Martin DB3S (engine),
with Peter Collins
April
2 Glover Trophy, Goodwood

1st in Maserati 250F; Sports Car Race
1st in Aston Martin DB3S
14 British Empire Trophy, Oulton Park
4th in heat in works 'Bobtail' Cooper-
Climax, 1st in final
23 Aintree 200
1st in Maserati 250F; Sports Car race,
5th in own 'Bobtail' Cooper-Climax
29 Mille Miglia, Italy
Ret'd in Maserati 350S (accident), with
Denis Jenkinson
May
5 BRDC International Trophy,
Silverstone
1st in Vanwall; Sports Car race,
2nd in Aston Martin DB3S
13 Monaco GP, Monte Carlo
1st in Maserati 250F
21 Crystal Palace, London Trophy,
Formula Libre
1st heat 1 in Maserati 250F, 1st in heat
2, 1st on aggregate; Anerley Trophy,
2nd in 'Bobtail' Cooper-Climax;
Norbury Trophy, 1st in 'Bobtail'
Cooper-Climax
27 Nürburgring 1000kms, Germany
1st in Maserati 300S, with Jean Behra,
having taken over Maserati 300S of
Taruffi/Schell
June
3 Belgian GP, Spa-Francorchamps
3rd in Maserati 250F
24 Supercortemaggiore GP, Monza, Italy
2nd in Maserati 150S, with Cesare
Perdisa, having taken over Maserati
200S
30 Reims 12-Hours, France
Ret'd in Cooper-Climax (overheating),
with Phil Hill
July
1 French GP, Reims-Gueux
5th in Maserati 250F, having taken over
Perdisa's Maserati 250F
8 Rouen GP, Les Essarts, France
2nd in Aston Martin DB3S
14 British GP, Silverstone
Ret'd in Maserati 250F (gearbox);
Sports Car race,
1st in Maserati 300S
22 Bari Sports Car GP, Italy
1st in Maserati 300S
28/29 Le Mans, France
2nd in Aston Martin DB3S, with Peter
Collins
August
5 German GP, Nürburgring
2nd in Maserati 250F; 1500cc Sports
Car race, 2nd in Maserati 150S
12 Swedish Sports Car GP, Rabelov
Ret'd in Maserati 300S (caught fire in
pits), with Jean Behra, took over
Villoresi/Schell Maserati 300S, ret'd
(brakes failed)
18 Daily Herald Trophy, Oulton Park
1st in Aston Martin DB3S; Sporting Life
Trophy, 1st in Les Leston 'Bobtail'
Cooper-Climax
September
2 Italian GP, Monza
1st in Maserati 250F
3 Monza Record breaking
50Kms 135.54mph, 50 miles
132.77mph in Lotus 11
17/23 Tour de France
2nd in Mercedes-Benz 300SL, with

George Huel
November
4 Venezuelan GP, Caracas
1st in Maserati 300S
25 Australian Tourist Trophy, Albert Park, Melbourne
1st in Maserati 300S
December
2 Australian GP, Melbourne
1st in Maserati 250F
9 Nassau Trophy, Windsor Field, Bahamas
1st in Bill Lloyd Maserati 300S

1957
January
13 Argentine GP, Buenos Aires
8th in Maserati 250F
20 Buenos Aires 1,000kms
2nd in Maserati 450S, with Fangio, having taken over Behra/Menditéguy Maserati 300S
27 Buenos Aires City GP
Ret'd in heat 1 in Maserati 250F (heat exhaustion), 6th in heat 2, having taken over Menditéguy Maerati 250F
February
24 Cuban GP Malecon Highway, Havana
Ret'd in Ettore Chimeri's Maserati 200S (engine), ret'd in Pinhero Pines' Maserati 300S (engine), having taken it over from Schell
March
24 Sebring 12-Hours, USA
2nd in Maserati 300S, with Harry Schell
April
7 Syracuse GP, Sicily
3rd in Vanwall
22 Glover Trophy, Goodwood
Ret'd in Vanwall (throttle linkage)
May
12 Mille Miglia, Italy
Ret'd in Maserati 450S (brake pedal snapped off after 7 miles)
19 Monaco GP, Monte Carlo
Ret'd in Vanwall (accident)
26 Nürburgring 1000Kms, Germany
5th in Maserati 450S, with Fangio, having taken over Scarlatti Maserati 300S and Godia/Gould Maserati 450S
June
22/23 Le Mans 24-Hours, France
Ret'd in Maserati 450S Berlinetta (transmission)
July
20 British GP, Aintree
1st in Vanwall, having taken over Brooks Vanwall
August
4 German GP, Nürburgring
5th in Vanwall
11 Swedish Sports Car GP, Rabelow
1st in Maserati 450S, with Jean Behra/Harry Schell and 3rd in Maserati 300S, with Bonnier/Schell/Scarlatti
18 Pescara GP, Italy
1st in Vanwall
23 Record breaking, Bonneville, Utah, USA
In MG EX181
September
8 Italian GP, Monza
1st in Vanwall
15 Tour de France

4th in Mercedes-Benz 300SL with Peter Garnier
October
27 Moroccan GP, Casablanca
Practised only (Asian flu) in Vanwall
November
3 Venezuelan GP, Caracas
Ret'd in Maserati 450S (accident), ret'd having taken over Behra 450S
December
3 Nassau Tourist Trophy, Oakes Field, Bahamas
25th overall in Aston Martin DBR2, 5th in Class C
6 Governor's Trophy
4th in heat in Aston Martin DBR2, 4th in final
8 Nassau Memorial Trophy
1st in NART 3.5 Ferrari 290S; Nassau Trophy, 1st in Ferrari 290S

194
out of 497 races won

1958
January
19 Argentine GP, Buenos Aires
1st in 1.9 Cooper-Climax.
26 Buenos Aires 1000Kms
3rd overall in Porsche RSK, 1st in class, with Jean Behra
February
2 Buenos Aires City GP
ret'd in heat 1 in 1.9 Cooper-Climax (accident)
24 Cuban GP, Havana
1st in 4.1 Ferrari 335S
March
22 Sebring 12-Hours, USA
Ret'd in Aston Martin DBR1 (transmission), with Tony Brooks
April
7 Sussex Trophy, Goodwood
1st in Aston Martin DBR2; Glover Trophy, ret'd in 1.9 Cooper-Climax (stalled at start)
12 British Empire Trophy, Oulton Park
1st in heat 3 in Aston Martin DBR2, 1st in final
19 Aintree 200
1st in 1.9 Cooper-Climax
May
3 BRDC International Trophy, Silverstone
Ret'd in 2.01 Cooper-Climax (engine); Sports Car race, ret'd in Aston Martin DBR3 (engine)
11 Targa Florio, Madonie, Sicily
Ret'd in Aston Martin DBR1 (transmission), with Tony Brooks
18 Monaco GP, Monte Carlo
Ret'd in Vanwall (valve gear)
26 Dutch GP, Zandvoort
1st in Vanwall
June
1 Nürburgring 1000Kms, Germany
1st in Aston Martin DBR1, with Jack Brabham
15 Belgian GP, Spa-Francorchamps
Ret'd in Vanwall (over-revved)
21 Le Mans 24-Hours, France
Ret'd in Aston Martin DBR1 (engine), with Jack Brabham

29 Two Worlds Trophy, Monza
4th in heat 1 in Eldorado Maserati, 5th in heat 2, ret'd heat 3 (steering broke)
July
6 French GP, Reims
2nd in Vanwall; Coupe de Vitesse ret'd in Cooper-Climax F2
13 Vila Real Sports Car GP, Portugal
1st in Maserati 300S
19 British GP, Silverstone
Ret'd in Vanwall (engine); Sports Car race, 1st in Lister-Jaguar
20 Caen GP, Le Prairie, France
1st in 2.2 Cooper-Climax
August
3 German GP, Nürburgring
5th in Vanwall
10 Karlskoga Kannonloppet, Sweden
1st in Maserati 300S
16 Copenhagen GP, Roskilde Ring, Denmark
Ret'd in heat 1 in Maserati 300S (engine); 1st in heats 2 and 3 in JBW Maserati
17 Roskilde Ring
2nd in heat 1 in Maserati 300S, 1st in heats 2 and 3, 2nd overall
24 Portuguese GP, Oporto
1st in Vanwall
30 Kentish '100', Brands Hatch
2nd in part 1 in Cooper-Climax F2, 1st in part 2, 1st overall
September
7 Italian GP, Monza
Ret'd in Vanwall (gearbox)
13 RAC Tourist Trophy, Goodwood
1st in Aston Martin DBR1, with Tony Brooks
October
19 Moroccan GP, Casablanca
1st in Vanwall
November
30 Melbourne GP, Albert Park, Australia
1st in heat one in 2.01 Cooper-Climax, 1st in final

19
fastest F1 laps

1959
January
10 New Zealand GP, Ardmore
Unplaced in heat 2 in 2.2 Cooper-Climax; Grand Prix 1st
March
21 Sebring 12-Hours, USA
Disqualified in Lister-Jaguar, with Ivor Bueb, took over & 15th in Cunningham/Underwood Lister-Jaguar
30 Glover Trophy, Goodwood
1st in 2.5 Cooper-Climax
April
8 GP d'Europe des Micromills, Paris, France
1st in heats 1 & 2, heat 3 ret'd (broken back axle), final 2nd, 1st overall
18 Aintree 200
Ret'd in Cooper-BRM (transmission)
24 Syracuse GP, Sicily
1st in Cooper-Borgward
May

2 BRDC International Trophy, Silverstone
Ret'd in BRM P25 (brake failure); GT race, 1st in Aston Martin DB4GT; Sports Car Race,
2nd in Aston Martin DBR1
10 Monaco GP, Monte Carlo
Ret'd in 2.5 Cooper-Climax (transmission)
31 Dutch GP, Zandvoort
Ret'd in 2.5 Cooper-Climax (transmission)
June
7 Nürburgring 1000Kms, Germany
1st in Aston Martin DBR1, with Jack Fairman
20/21 Le Mans 24 Hours, France
Ret'd in Aston Martin DBR1, with Jack Fairman (engine)
July
7 French GP, Reims-Gueux
Ret'd in BRM P25 (spun & stalled); F2 Coupe de Vitesse, 1st in Cooper-Borgward
12 Rouen GP, Les Essarts, France
1st in Cooper-Borgward; Coupe Delamere Deboutteville,
1st in Maserati Tipo 60
18 British GP, Aintree
2nd in BRM P25; Sports Car race, ret'd in Cooper-Monaco (caught fire)
26 Circuit d'Auvergne, Clermont, France
1st in Cooper-Borgward
August
2 German GP, AVUS, Berlin
Ret'd in heat 1 in 2.5 Cooper-Climax (transmission)
9 Karlskoga Kannonloppet, Sweden
1st in Cooper Monaco
15/16 Copenhagen GP, Roskildering, Denmark
1st in heat 1 in Cooper Monaco, 2nd in heat 2, 2nd in heat 3, 1st overall on aggregate
23 Portuguese GP, Monsanto, Lisbon
1st in 2.5 Cooper-Climax
29 F2 Kentish '100', Brands Hatch, GB
3rd in heat 1 in Cooper-Borgward, 4th in heat 2, 3rd overall on aggregate
September
5 RAC Tourist Trophy, Goodwood
1st in Aston Martin DBR1, with Tony Brooks, having taken over Shelby/Fairman Aston Martin DBR1
13 Italian GP, Monza
1st in 2.5 Cooper-Climax
26 Oulton Park Gold Cup
1st in 2.5 Cooper-Climax
October
10/11 LA Times GP, Riverside, USA
Ret'd in Aston Martin DBR2 (overheating & low oil pressure)
18 Watkins Glen Libre GP, USA
1st in 2.5 Cooper-Climax
November
29 Nassau Tourist Trophy
1st in over 2-litre heat in Aston Martin DB4GT, ret'd in final (engine)
December
4 Governor's Trophy over 2-litre race
1st in heat in Aston Martin DBR2, 1st in final
6 Nassau Trophy race
Ret'd in Aston Martin DBR2 (brake disc sheared)

12 United States GP, Sebring
Ret'd in 2.5 Cooper-Climax
(transmission)

1960

January
1 South African GP, East London
2nd in Cooper-Borgward
9 New Zealand GP, Ardmore
1st in heat in 2.5 Cooper-Climax, ret'd
in GP (clutch)
31 Go-Kart race, Nassau
2nd

February
7 Argentine GP, Buenos Aires
3rd in 2.5 Cooper-Climax
28 Cuban GP, Havana
1st in Maserati Tipo 61

March
19 Syracuse GP, Sicily
Ret'd in F2 Porsche (engine)
25 Sebring 4-Hours, USA
2nd in Austin-Healey Sprite
26 Sebring 12-Hours
Ret'd in Maserati Tipo 61, with Dan
Gurney (transmission)

April
10 Brussels GP, Heysel, Belgium
1st in heat 1 in F2 Porsche, 3rd in heat
2, 2nd overall on aggregate points
18 Glover Trophy, Goodwood
2nd in 2.5 Cooper-Climax; Lavant Cup
2nd in F2 Porsche; Fordwater Trophy
1st in Aston Martin DB4GT
30 Aintree 200
1st in F2 Porsche

May
14 BRDC International Trophy,
Silverstone
Ret'd in 2.5 Cooper-Climax (wishbone);
Touring Car race,
2nd in 3.8 Jaguar Mark 2
22 Nürburgring 1000Kms, Germany
1st in Maserati Tipo 61
29 Monaco GP, Monte Carlo
1st in Lotus-Climax 18

June
6 Dutch GP, Zandvoort
4th in Lotus-Climax 18
12 Go-Kart race, Long Marston
1st
18 Belgian GP, Spa-Francorchamps
Crashed in practice in Lotus-Climax 18

August
7 Karlskoga Kannonloppet, Sweden
1st in Lotus Climax 19
14 Portuguese GP, Oporto
Disqualified in Lotus-Climax 18
20 RAC Tourist Trophy, Goodwood
1st in Ferrari 250GT SWB
21 Go-Kart race
2nd
27 F2 Kentish '100', Brands Hatch
11th in F2 Porsche; Redex Trophy,
1st in Ferrari 250GT SWB

September
10/11 Copenhagen GP, Roskildering,
Denmark
4th in two heats in F2 Porsche, 3rd in
another, 4th overall on aggregate
18 Austrian GP, Zeltweg
1st in F2 Porsche
24 Oulton Park Gold Cup
1st in Lotus-Climax 18

October

2 Modena GP, Italy
Ret'd in F2 Lotus-Climax 18 (valvegear)
9 Watkins Glen Libre GP, USA
1st in Lotus-Climax 18
16 LA Times GP, Riverside, USA
Ret'd in Lotus-Climax 19
(transmission)
23 Pacific GP, Laguna Seca, USA
1st in heat 1 in Lotus-Climax 19, 1st in
heat 2

November
20 United States GP, Riverside
1st in Lotus-Climax 18
24/25 Go-Kart race
13th
27 Nassau Tourist Trophy, Oakes Field,
Bahamas
1st in Ferrari 250GT SWB

December
3 Governor's Trophy
Ret'd in Lotus-Climax 19
4 Nassau Trophy
Ret'd in Lotus-Climax 19 (front
suspension)
17 Cape GP, Killarney, South Africa
1st in F2 Porsche
27 South African GP, East London
1st in F2 Porsche

62
races in one year

1961

January
7 New Zealand GP, Ardmore
1st in heat, ret'd in final in 2.5 Lotus-
Climax 18 (half-shaft)
21 Lady Wigram Trophy, Christchurch,
New Zealand
2nd in 2.5 Lotus-Climax 18
29 Australian GP (InterContinental
race), Warwick Farm, Sydney
1st in 2.5 Lotus-Climax 18

March
24 Sebring 4-Hours, Florida, USA
4th in Austin-Healey Sprite
25 Florida International 12-Hour GP of
Endurance, Sebring
Ret'd in Maserati T 61, with Graham Hill
(exhaust), took over & ret'd in Maserati
T63, with Masten Gregory (rear
suspension)

April
3 Easter Monday, Goodwood
Lavant Cup (InterContinental race),
1st in 2.5 Cooper-Climax T53P; Glover
Trophy,
4th in 1.5 Lotus-Climax 18; Sussex
Trophy,
1st in Lotus-Climax 19; Fordwater
Trophy,
3rd in Aston Martin DB4 GTZ
9 Brussels GP, Heysel, Belgium
Unclassified in heat 1, 8th in heat 2,
2nd in final heat, unclassified overall
but unofficially 7th in 1.5 Lotus-Climax
18
16 Vienna Preis, Aspern, Austria
1st 1.5 Lotus-Climax 18
22 Aintree 200
Ret'd in 1.5 Cooper-Climax (engine);
Sports Car race,

1st in UDT/Laystall Lotus-Climax 19
25 Syracuse GP
Ret'd in 1.5 Lotus-Climax 18 (magneto)
30 Targa Florio, Tribune do Cerda,
Madonie, Sicily
Ret'd in Porsche RS60 1.9, with Graham
Hill (transmission)

May
6 BRDC International Trophy,
Silverstone
Inter-Continental race, 1st in 2.5
Cooper-Climax T53P; Sports Car race,
1st in Lotus-Climax 19
14 Monaco GP, Monte-Carlo
1st in 1.5 Lotus-Climax 18
22 Dutch GP, Zandvoort, The
Netherlands
4th in 1.5 Lotus-Climax 18
28 1,000 Kms, Nürburgring, Germany
Ret'd in Porsche RS61 1.7, with Graham
Hill, took over Porsche Carrera, with
Linge & Gregor, 8th overall and 1st in
2-litre class

June
3 Silver City Trophy, Brands Hatch
1st in UDT/Laystall 1.5 Lotus-Climax
18/21
10/11 Le Mans 24-Hours, France
Ret'd in Ferrari 250 GT, with Graham
Hill (fan)
18 Belgian GP, Spa-Francorchamps
8th in Lotus-Climax 18/21
24 Players 200, Mosport, Canada
1st in heat 1, 1st in heat 2, 1st on
aggregate in Lotus-Climax 19

July
2 French GP, Reims
Ret'd in 1.5 Lotus-Climax 18/21
(accident)
8 British Empire Trophy, Silverstone
Inter-Continental race; 1st in 2.5
Cooper-Climax T53P; GT race,
1st in Ferrari 250GT SWB
15 British GP, Aintree
Ret'd in Lotus-Climax 18/21 (brake
pipe), took over & disqualified in 4WD
Ferguson-Climax P99
23 Solitude GP, Stuttgart, Germany
Ret'd in UDT/Laystall 1.5 Lotus-Climax
18/21

August
6 European GP (German GP),
Nürburgring, Germany
1st in Lotus-Climax 18/21
7 Brands Hatch, Kent
Peco Trophy,
1st in Ferrari 250GT SWB; Guards
Trophy Inter-Continental race,
ret'd in 2.5 Cooper-Climax T53P
(transmission)
19 RAC Tourist Trophy, Goodwood
1st in Ferrari 250GT SWB
20 Karlskoga Kannonloppet, Sweden
1st in UDT/Laystall Lotus 18/21
26/27 Danish GP, Roskilde, Denmark
1st in three heats and 1st on overall
aggregate in UDT/Laystall 1.5 Lotus-
Climax 18/21

September
3 Modena GP, Italy
1st in 1.5 Lotus-Climax 18/21 (V8
Climax)
10 Italian GP, Monza, Italy
Ret'd in Team Lotus Works Lotus-
Climax 21 (wheel bearing)

23 Oulton Park Gold Cup, Cheshire
1st in Ferguson-Climax P99
30 Canadian GP, Mosport Park
3rd in Lotus-Climax 19

October
8 United States GP, Watkins Glen
Ret'd in Lotus-Climax 18/21 (4-cyl)
(engine)
13-15 LA Times GP, Riverside, USA
16th in Lotus-Climax 19; 3-Hour
Production Car race,
3rd overall and 1st in class in Sunbeam
Alpine, with Jack Brabham
22 Pacific GP, Laguna Seca, Monterey,
USA
1st in heat 1, 1st in heat 2 and 1st
overall on aggregate in Lotus-Climax
19

December
3-12 Nassau Tourist Trophy, Bahamas
1st in heat, 1st in final in Ferrari 250GT
SWB; Governor's Trophy, ret'd in heat
in Team Rosebud Lotus-Climax 19;
Nassau Trophy, ret'd in Lotus- Climax
19 (rear wishbone)
17 Natal GP, Westmead, Durban, South
Africa
2nd in UDT/Laystall 1.5 Lotus-Climax
18/21
26 South African GP, East London
2nd in UDT/Laystall 1.5 Lotus-Climax
18/21

01
point separating
Moss and 1958 F1
champion Hawthorn

1962

January
6 New Zealand GP, Ardmore
1st in 2.5 Lotus-Climax 21
13 Vic Hudson Memorial, Levin, NZ
2nd in heat in 2.7 Cooper-Climax, 2nd
in final
20 Lady Wigram Trophy, Christchurch,
New Zealand
1st in 2.5 Lotus Climax 21
27 Teretonga Trophy, Invercargill, NZ
2nd in heat 1 in 2.7 Cooper-Climax, 2nd
in final

February
4 Warwick Farm 100, Sydney, Australia
1st in 2.7 Cooper-Climax
11 Daytona Continental, USA
1st in GT class & 4th overall in Ferrari
250GT Speciale

March
23 Sebring 3-Hours, USA
3rd in Austin-Healey Sprite
25 Sebring 12-Hours, USA
Disqualified in Ferrari 250TR/61, with
Innes Ireland

April
1 Brussels GP, Heysel, Belgium
2nd in heat 1 in Lotus-Climax 18/21 V8,
ret'd in heat 2 (engine)
14 Lombank Trophy, Snetterton
7th in Lotus-Climax 18/21 V8
23 Glover Trophy, Goodwood
Ret'd in Lotus-Climax 18/21 V8
(accident)

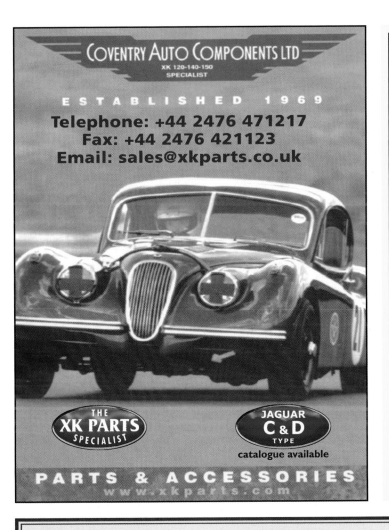

Attention ANORAKS

Famously, Stirling Moss is regarded as the greatest driver never to have won the World Championship. But how might he have fared if his cars had been as reliable as today's F1 racers?
Words: Philip Porter

As an amusing little exercise, I have attempted to apply today's reliability to the results of Stirling's seasons from 1955 to 1961, and then computed these 'results' with today's points system.

It was always said that Moss suffered immense bad luck in his career. So often he was leading and had the measure of the field, when some minor component let the side down and yet another gallant drive was foiled. For a short while he was tarred with the charge of being a car-breaker. This was quickly and entirely demolished by Rob Walker for whose team he drove.

In recent years, reliability in racing has almost become a given. Gone are the days when half the entry fails, other than when freak conditions apply. The weather, a major accident or a series of incidents have been known to wreak havoc but more normally we see a procession of reliable cars. Indeed, analysing the results of the World Champion drivers from 2001 to 2008, we find Schumacher retired twice in 2001, not at all in 2003, and once each in 2003 and 2004. Alonso failed to finish twice in each of his Championship years, as did Raikkonen in 2007, while Hamilton had a clean sheet in 2008. That amounts to 14 retirements in 140 races, or, rather obviously, a retirement every 10 races.

For the purpose of this lighthearted look at Stirling's results, I have assumed this decade's level of reliability; that is, almost 100%. As the seasons were much shorter in the '50s and '60s, one in 10 would equate to, roughly, one retirement every other season. If I was to apply that selectively, I could easily distort the figures to Stirling's advantage by deducting one of his lowest scoring races and one of his closest rival's best results. I have attempted to apply complete reliability to the leading contenders, and not just to Moss.

For an extra bit of fun, I have also applied the old system of counting only the best five (best six in 1958 and 1960) and also used that basis with the old, period scoring system.

Below
Stirling Moss's big breakthrough in the international arena of Grand Prix racing, and the opportunity to show his true ability, came about when he was invited to join the Mercedes-Benz team for their second season in 1955.

Right
Moss spent most of the 1955 season driving his W196 in close company with that of team leader, Juan Manuel Fangio, to such an extent that they became known as 'the train'.

1955

In 1955 Moss was still learning his craft and was number two to World Champion, Juan Manuel Fangio. A mixture of respect and team orders meant that Stirling did not challenge his team leader. As a consequence, the reliability factor does not impact greatly on this season.

Fangio won the Argentine GP, but Moss retired when second. At Monaco, they both retired, first Fangio while leading and then Moss while out in front, but as Fangio went out first, he would have been the winner with Moss second. That was how they actually finished in Holland. In Britain, Stirling famously beat his team leader by a few feet. Fangio won the final event, the Italian GP, but Stirling, who was lying second, was delayed when a stone thrown by one of Fangio's wheels smashed his aero screen. This was a racing incident and therefore his sixth place stands.

Applying all this would not have affected the overall results with Fangio scoring 48 points to Stirling's 37, as opposed to the actual scores of 40 and 23 respectively.

1956

For 1956, Fangio went to Ferrari and Moss became team leader at rivals, Maserati. The opening race was once more the Argentine GP. Moss was leading when he retired which allowed Fangio to win, but only after he changed cars because he had blown up his own Lancia-Ferrari. It seems fair to give the win to Moss, and Fangio second place. At Monaco, Stirling led from flag to flag while Fangio crashed. At Spa Fangio, in the faster V8 Ferrari, overtook Moss, who then had the misfortune to lose a wheel.

At Reims, for the French GP, the Maseratis were again too slow and Moss retired when the gear lever snapped off. The British GP saw Moss leading Fangio until an ignition malfunction sent the Englishman into the pits. It is reasonable to suppose Stirling would have won. At the 'Ring, the two rivals traded fastest laps but Fangio won on the road, fair and square.

For the final Grand Prix of the season, the Italians, Castellotti and Musso, wrecked their tyres by dicing early on and when they had to pit for fresh rubber, Stirling was able to take over the lead. Fangio followed him in second position.

So, how do they end the season on this basis? Fangio would have scored 47 points to Moss's total of 54. Stirling would have been World Champion with three wins to the actual champion's two. On the basis of the best five results, Moss would have taken it with 46 to 42 and under the old period scoring system he would have had 36 to 32.

Above
Moss' Maserati, carrying his trademark number seven, finished second to Fangio's Ferrari at the Nürburgring in 1956.

Below
By the harbour wall at Monte Carlo as Moss deftly pilots his Maserati to victory in the 1956 Monaco Grand Prix.

1957

The season opened again with the Argentine GP. Though Stirling had signed for Vanwall for 1957, they decided not to contest this race and so Moss had a works 250F Maser. He was fastest in practice from Fangio by over a second but then had to pit at the end of the first lap, losing nine laps on the leaders. He set fastest lap and made up a whole one on Fangio so it is reasonable to assume he would have won that event, given complete reliability. At Monaco, in the Vanwall, he was leading when the brakes failed. Fangio went on to

take the chequered flag, but would probably have been second otherwise

Stirling missed the French GP due to a nasty nasal infection, and Fangio cashed in. In the British GP, Moss was leading in his own car before it succumbed and he took over Tony Brooks' Vanwall. Fangio was sixth when he retired. However, he was supreme in Germany while the Vanwalls were a disaster on the bumpy track. The Argentine won and Moss could only manage fifth.

At Pescara, Stirling was in a class of his

own and Fangio a distant second, more than three minutes behind. In Italy, they again finished one-two.

Fangio was once again crowned World Champion and on the total reliability basis, he would have taken it by a point, even though he only had two wins to Moss' five. Missing that French GP proved crucial. **However, applying the best five scenario would have seen Stirling scoring 50 points to Fangio's 44, and under the period scoring he would have amassed 40 to the 34 of Fangio.**

Left
Fangio had one of the greatest drives of his life to win the 1957 German Grand Prix, utterly overshadowing Moss. Stirling's Vanwall could only manage fifth place.

Below
The Vanwalls found themselves ill-suited to the Nürburgring in 1957. Moss' number 10 car achieved fifth, Tony Brooks was ninth and Stuart Lewis-Evans failed to finish thanks to gearbox trouble on lap 10.

1958

This was the year when Fangio retired during the season and Mike Hawthorn became the first Englishman to win the World title, even though he only actually won one race, beating Stirling by a crucial single point.

Stirling was to drive for Vanwall in 1958 but, once again, they decided not to make the trip to the season-opening Argentine GP. As recounted elsewhere, Stirling drove a little rear-engined Cooper and took a remarkable first victory for the marque. Hawthorn was third. Moss was leading from Hawthorn at Monaco when his Vanwall's engine failed. Hawthorn also retired but it is fair to assume he would have finished second. Stirling won the Dutch GP with Hawthorn fifth, a lap down.

In the Belgium GP, Moss retired due to a rare mistake when he over-revved. As this was self-induced, as opposed to bad luck, he scores no points. Hawthorn was second.

The French event was Mike's only win and Stirling was runner-up, though he had to contend with a misfiring engine, a left front brake locking, trailing smoke and the loss of second and third gears. He only inherited second when Behra retired so, on the reliability basis, he is placed third, though you could argue he would have done rather better without all his handicaps!

Pete Collins, in his penultimate GP, won the British race and Stirling was five seconds behind until his engine threw a rod. Moss was easily leading the German GP when he retired with a small screw adrift in the magneto. Without retirements, including his own, Hawthorn would probably have finished third, due to Collins's very sad fatal accident.

In Portugal, Stirling and Mike finished first and second on the road, as they also did in the season's exciting finale in Morocco.

It is perhaps less surprising that Moss finishes ahead on the adjusted points basis in 1958 though the margin is actually quite small – 74 to 72, in spite of him 'having' six wins to Hawthorn's one. It broadens on the other basis – 60 to 42 on the best six results and 48 to 32 on the best six with the old scoring of 8, 6, 4, 3, 2, 1.

Above
Not even the lucky number seven would allow a British success for Moss and his Vanwall at Aintree in 1958. He retired after 25 laps.

Left
Monaco in 1958 proved another disappointing race for Vanwall, with Moss' car suffering engine problems on lap 38.

Below
Moss and Hawthorne dominated the 1958 Portuguese Grand Prix. Here, Hawthorne's Ferrari is leading Moss' Vanwall although, by the end of the race, these positions would be reversed.

1959

Stirling was now driving for Rob Walker's private team in their Cooper-Climaxes and his main rival was to be Australian Jack Brabham in the works Cooper. At Monaco, Moss led from lap 22 until, with 19 of the 100 laps to go, he retired with transmission problems. The Colotti gearbox was to blight his season. Brabham was in second place, some 40 seconds down the road. Stirling made a bad start in the Dutch GP but worked his way up to the front when, with 15 laps to go, the Colotti failed again. Brabham, at that point, was third, Jo Bonnier taking the honours that day for BRM's first win at long, long last.

In the French GP, Moss chose to drive a BRM while Rob Walker's team attempted to sort out their transmission problems. It was a hot day and unfortunately Stirling spun on the melted tar, after he had driven superbly with a broken clutch and was challenging for second place. It could be argued that he would not have spun but for his clutch problems but, perhaps harshly, we will put that one down to driver error. Brooks in the Ferrari was unbeatable that day and Brabham came third.

The BRM was Stirling's mount in the British GP and, with a slipping clutch, he finished second to Jack. The next GP was the German, at the fearsome AVUS circuit, on which the three front-engined Ferraris dominated due to their high maximum speed. Stirling, now back in the Cooper, was second when he retired with the usual transmission problems and Brabham also dropped out later in the race.

In the Portuguese GP, the Colotti gearbox finally did the business and Stirling won, whereas his chief rival crashed. In Italy, Moss made it two in a row and Brabham was third. The Championship for real came down to the US race. Stirling led, until his transmission, yet again, ruined his chances. Brabham finished fifth - it would have been sixth if Moss had not retired - but had enough points to take the title.

On our basis, Jack would have taken one win to Stirling's five and amassed 40 points to Stirling's 66. As to the best five, the Englishman would have totalled 50 against 36, or, with period points some 40 to 26.

Above
Moss only just won the 1959 New Zealand Grand Prix, having to push his Cooper T45 Climax over the finish line.

Below
Close action racing at the 1959 Dutch Grand Prix with Graham Hill, Harry Schell and Stirling Moss bringing up the rear in his Cooper-Climax.

Right
Moss was leading the 1959 Monaco event right up until lap 81 when the unreliable Colotti transmission failed on his Cooper-Climax and he was forced to retire.

1960

This season was not a happy one for Moss. He would have won in the Argentine and did win in Monaco. He was fourth in Holland and then had his massive accident at Spa when a wheel fell off the Lotus 18. He missed three GPs out of a total of nine. Even Stirling Moss could not overcome that handicap.

1961

This was to be another challenging year. The British teams had not believed the new 1½-litre engine limit would be adopted and were totally unprepared when it arrived. Ferrari, on the other hand, were on the ball and their powerful V6 engines and their distinctive shark-nosed cars were ready to do battle. They also had a strong team with Americans, Phil Hill and Richie Ginther, and German aristocrat, Count 'Taffy' von Trips, plus assorted others from time to time, fielding no less than six cars for the crucial Italian GP. Furthermore, due to contractual restraints imposed by their sponsors, Esso, Lotus were not allowed to sell to Rob Walker their latest 21, a car that a future star by the name of Jim Clark would have at his disposal. Stirling liked to be the underdog but the odds were really stacking up against him.

Having said all that, he turned in one of the finest drives of his career to win the Monaco GP on a circuit where skill, not just outright power, were crucial. Ginther, Hill and von Trips occupied the next three places. At Zandvoort, for the Dutch GP, Stirling could do no better than fourth and von Trips took the flag, followed by Hill. For probably the only time in his career, Moss had an off day at Spa, allowing Hill to head von Trips.

At Reims, Stirling was lying third when his brakes started playing up, leading to his retirement. The Ferrari of von Trips would

have won but his engine let him down. Then Hill spun, Ginther retired and the fourth Ferrari of Giancarlo Baghetti, driving in his first GP, won. The British GP, at Aintree, had appalling conditions which helped Stirling, who ran second for a while before spinning and losing a place. He then retired with brake maladies. Hill was second to von Trips.

In Germany, Stirling was once again able to show his complete mastery on a damp Nürburgring track. With skill again paramount, Moss was supreme. Sadly, the popular German von Trips's run was to come to an end at Monza when he crashed fatally. As Moss had a slender chance of taking the Championship, Innes Ireland, with an incredibly sporting gesture, gave Stirling his works Lotus 21 to drive. Hill won the race and without his own and various retirements ahead of him, it is likely Moss would have finished fourth. Hill's win gave him the Championship and so Ferrari did not contest the US GP, which Moss led until he retired with no oil pressure.

Ferrari giving the last race a miss makes any conclusions open to debate. On the basis of reliability, Moss and von Trips tied on points and with three wins apiece, with Hill three points adrift. On the best five basis, they again tied, with Hill four points behind. Applying the old scoring system, it would have gone to 'Taffy' von Trips.

Conclusion

So, there we are. If we take luck out of the equation and base the Championship on actual performance rather than the reliability lottery of those days, concentrating on skill, racecraft and determination, we see that Stirling Moss might well have been World Champion several times. Having said that, he is proud to be remembered, as others have described him, as 'the greatest driver never to have won the World Championship.'

In reality, whatever statistics might or might not tell us and however fairly we may try to apply them, we all know that Stirling Moss, taking Grand Prix racing, sports cars, touring cars and rally cars into account, was the greatest all-round racing driver the world has yet seen.

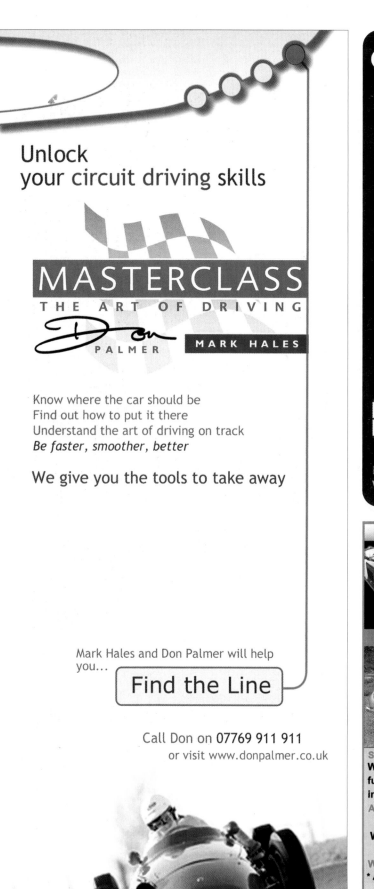

Every
CAR MOSS RACED

Sir Stirling estimated it at 80 cars, but in fact we make it 107 that he raced during his professional career, from rally cars to Formula Ones

Racing drivers have had longer careers. With nearly 20 Grands Prix a year, today's drivers have competed in far more Formula One races. There are people, such as Gerry Marshall, Mike Salmon and 'Whizzo' Williams who have clocked up far more victories in motor racing at many levels.

It is questionable, though, whether any topline F1 pilot and prolific Grand Prix winner has ever driven so many different cars in anger as Stirling Moss. These include rally cars, touring cars, trials cars, sports cars, sports racing cars, record-breaking cars, Formula Junior cars, Formula Two cars and, of course, Formula One cars. The diversity is extraordinary.

Here we have gathered, possibly for the first time ever, what we believe is a comprehensive and complete illustrated listing of all the cars Sir Stirling drove between 1947 and 1962.

Even Sir Stirling was surprised when we gave him the total. We make it 107 used in competition and we have thrown in three more for good measure that he drove in testing, for publicity or for demonstration purposes. We have not treated the same car he drove for different teams, but have included the three variations of C-type Jaguar because they were distinctly altered cars for each of the three years they appeared at Le Mans.

By any criteria, it is an amazing list – a measure of the man's remarkable versatility.

1947 BMW 328

1948 Cooper-JAP 500 Mark II

1949 Cooper-JAP 500 Mark III

1950 Cooper-MG

1950 Cooper-Norton 500 Mark V

1950/1 Jaguar XK 120 Open Two Seater

1950/1/2 Kieft-Norton 500

1951 Morris Minor

1951/2 HWM Formula Two

1952 Harford III

1952 Jaguar XK 120 Fixed Head Coupé

1952/3/4 Jaguar Mark VII

1952 Cooper-Norton Mark VI

1952/3 Connaught A-type

1952 Humber Super Snipe 15 countries run

1953 Jaguar C-type Lightweight

1953 Cooper-Alta Mark II

1953 Cooper-JAP 1100 Mark VII

1949 Cooper-JAP Mark III 1000

1950 HWM

1950 Cooper-JAP 500 Mark IV

1950/1/2 Frazer Nash Le Mans Replica

1950 Aston Martin DB2

1950 Kieft-Norton 350

1951 Jaguar C-type

1951 Ferrari 166 practised only

1952/3/4 Sunbeam Talbot 90

1952 BRM V16

1952 Jaguar C-type Long-nose

1952 ERA G-type

1953/4 Sunbeam-Talbot Alpine

1953 Cooper-Alta

1953 Cooper-Norton 500 Mark VII

1954 OSCA MT4

1954 Leonard-MG

1954 Beart-Cooper 500 Mark VIIA

1954/5/6/7 Maserati 250F

1954 Jaguar D-type

1954 Lister-Bristol

1955 Beart-Climax

1955 Mercedes-Benz 300SLR

1955/6 Porsche 550

1956 Cooper T39 Mark II 'Bobtail'

1956 Maserati 350S

1956/7/8 Vanwall

1956/7 Mercedes-Benz 300SL Gullwing

1956 W.M.-Cooper-Holden demo only

1957 Maserati 450S

1957 Ferrari 290S

1958 Cooper-Climax 1.9 Formula One

1958 Porsche 550A

1958 Aston Martin DBR3/300

1958 Maserati Eldorado Special

1958 Cooper-Climax T45 Formula Two

1954 Connaught ALSR

1955 Mercedes-Benz W196

1955 Austin-Healey 100S

1955 Standard 10

1956/7/8 Maserati 300S

1956 Aston Martin DB3S

1956 Maserati 150S

1956/7 Maserati 200S

1956 Lotus XI

1957 Maserati 450S Berlinetta

1957 MG EX.181

1957/8/9 Aston Martin DBR2

1958 Ferrari 335S

1958/9 Aston Martin DBR1/300

1958 Cooper-Climax 2.01 Formula One

1958 Lister-Jaguar Knobbly

1958/9 Cooper-Climax 2.2 Formula One

1958 JBW-Maserati

1959 Lister-Jaguar Costin

1959/60 Cooper-Climax 2.5 Formula One

1959 Micromill

1959/60 Aston Martin DB4GT

1959 Maserati Tipo 60 Birdcage

1959 Cooper-Monaco

1960 Jaguar 3.8 Mark II

1960/1 Lotus-Climax 18 2.5 Formula One

1960/1 Lotus-Climax 19 Monte Carlo

1961 Cooper-Climax T53P 2.5 InterContinental

1961 Lotus-Climax 18 1.5 Formula One

1961 Cooper-Climax 1.5 Formula One

1961 Porsche Carrera

1961 Lotus Climax 18/21 1.5 Formula One

1961 Ferrari 250GT SWB Compezione

1961 Sunbeam Alpine

1962 Lotus-Climax 21 2.5

1962 Cooper-Climax T53P 2.7 InterContinental

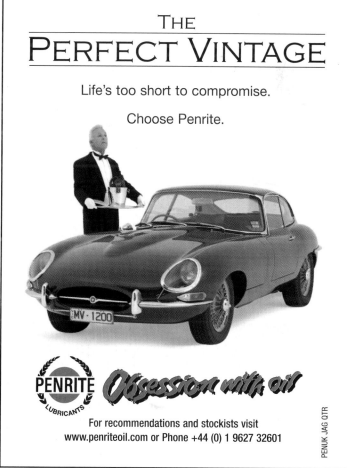

1959 Cooper-BRM

1959/60 Cooper-Borgward Formula Two

1959 BRM P25

1960/1 Maserati Tipo 61 Birdcage

1960 Porsche F2-718

1960/1/2 Austin-Healey Sprite

1960 Ferrari 250GT SWB

1960 Various Go-karts

1961 Maserati Tipo 63 rear-engine

1961 Aston Martin DB4GT Zagato

1961 Porsche RS60 1.9

1961 Porsche RS61 1.7

1961 Lotus-Climax 21 1.5 Formula One

1961/2 Lotus Climax 18/21 1.5 V8 Formula One

1961 Ferguson-Climax P99 1.5 Formula One

1962 Ferrari 250GT Speciale

1962 Ferrari 250 Testa Rossa/61

1961/62 Ferrari 250GTO Prototype